ROCK SOLID GOLF

A FOUNDATION FOR A LIFETIME

ADVANCE PRAISE FOR ROCK SOLID GOLF

Not only is Dana Rader one of the best teachers
of our game in the country, she is one of the
finest, most positive people I have ever known.

Mike Purkey
Senior Editor, GOLF *Magazine*

Dana Rader makes the maddening pursuit of
hitting a golf ball fun. She has the ability to analyze
a golf swing, and more importantly, she can
explain what works and what doesn't.

Ron Green, Jr.
Golf Editor, *The Charlotte Observer*

I've always been impressed with Dana Rader
as a player and as a teacher. Now, I'm equally
impressed with her as an author. Read
Rock Solid Golf. It's a rare find.

Harry Nicholas
North Carolina Golf Panel

Rock Solid Golf progresses logically, chapter by chapter, in an easy to understand and often entertaining style. Get the book. It will help you find the right answers for change in your game.

Dr. Gary Wiren
PGA Master Professional; Founder &
Chairman, Golf Around the World

Rock Solid Golf is the perfect title for Dana Rader's book as her understanding of the golf swing and her ability to communicate those mechanics could only be described as "rock solid."

Lorin Anderson
Managing Editor, GOLF Magazine

One reason golf is the outstanding game it is, is because of people like Dana Rader.

Peggy Kirk Bell
Member, LPGA Teaching Hall of Fame
Recipient, USGA Bob Jones Award

ROCK SOLID GOLF

A FOUNDATION FOR A LIFETIME

FIRST EDITION

BY DANA RADER
with Scott Martin

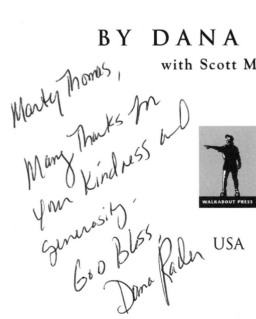

Marty Thomas,
Many Thanks for
Your kindness and
Generosity.
God Bless,
Dana Rader

Sept. 06

WALKABOUT PRESS

USA

Walkabout Press, Inc.
P.O. Box 11329
Charlotte, NC 28220-1329

Find us online at **www.walkaboutpress.com**

Copyright © 2003 by Walkabout Press, Inc.

ISBN: 1-931339-08-2
Library of Congress Control Number: 2002110909

Library of Congress Cataloguing-in-Publication Data is available.

Editors: Malcolm Campbell; Ryan Croxton
Cover & Interior Design: Trudy Lampley Designs

Interior photographs by James J. Bissell, unless otherwise noted.
Front cover photograph © Jim Noble, 1996
Back cover, inside back flap, and Chapter 8 photographs by Jon Silla.

The publisher and author do not assume, and hereby disclaim, any liability for any loss or damage caused by errors, omissions, misleading information or problems experienced due to information contained in this book, even if such errors of omissions resulted from negligence, accident or any other cause. Furthermore, this book provides information about recreational activities, which by their nature, are potentially hazardous. In participating in any of the activities described herein, readers assume all risk of injury or loss that may occur as the result of participation in such activities.

Special Sales
Corporations, organizations, mail-order catalogs, institutions, and charities may make bulk purchases (15+ copies) of this book at special discounts. Walkabout Press can produce custom editions of this book for use as premiums or incentives in sales promotions. This content may be available for private label imprints. Contact Malcolm W. Campbell, Walkabout Press, P.O. Box 11329, Charlotte, NC 28220-1329, or call (704) 348-4467.

To my parents, my students, and
Julie Cole and Pat Walker, my sisters in Christ.

ACKNOWLEDGEMENTS

I dedicate this book first to all my students over the last 21 years and to the great city of Charlotte—a wonderful place to live and a growing and prosperous city that's both loyal and nurturing to entrepreneurs like myself.

I thank my father, Vernon Rader, and my mother, Jean, for their love and guidance and for encouraging me to follow my dreams. I especially thank my father for the strong principles he instilled in me at an early age.

I thank God for his Word, truth, and the joy that comes from a personal relationship with Jesus Christ—for in Him all things are possible, if you only believe.

I thank Julie Cole for her support and dedication to the Dana Rader Golf School. Her hard work, vision, and desire to be the very best is why we continue to grow the game of golf. I treasure her friendship as a blessed gift. I thank Jay Reid and Pat Walker—my first team at the Dana Rader Golf School—for their devotion to the school's success and their trust in God. They helped turn the vision into reality. I thank my entire staff at the Dana Rader Golf School and Ballantyne Resort for all you do. I will be eternally grateful for the support of Smoky Bissell, who believed in the idea and provided the school a home at his wonderful facility. Smoky is a man of true integrity, and I value his friendship. I thank David Conlan, my business mentor and friend. He generously offered his wisdom, guidance, and friendship. With his encouragement, I finally realized my dream of writing a book.

I would also like to thank Women's Golf Unlimited; Nancy Lopez and the incredible staff at the Nancy Lopez Company; Square Two; Lady Fairway; Jimmy Jones; George Nichols—a mentor and dear friend; Cindy Davis; Peggy Kirk Bell; Betsy Clark; Kerry Graham; Marge Burns; Annette Thompson; Carroll Johnson; Barrie Oringer at Golf for Women; Lee Siegel at The Golf Channel; Lorin Anderson at *GOLF Magazine*; Larry Mathe at EP Pro; and the LPGA Teaching and Club Professional Division. They have all helped me in many ways.

TABLE OF CONTENTS

Foreword by Nancy Lopez   xii

Preface   xv

Introduction   1

CHAPTER 1 **Misconceptions**   7
    Keep your head down
    Keep the right elbow tucked
    Don't sway; keep your head still
    Play the ball off the forward foot
    Misconceptions about the takeaway

CHAPTER 2 **The Fundamentals**   23
    Grip
    Posture & stance
    Ball position
    Alignment & target awareness

CHAPTER 3 **The Swing**   39
    The swing plane
    The Playing Zone
    The takeaway
    The middle of the backswing
    Top of the swing
    Downswing
    Impact
    Follow through
    Common swing errors

CHAPTER 4 *The Short Game*   **63**

The clock

Sand shots

Chipping

Pitching

Putting

CHAPTER 5 *The Pre-Shot Routine*   **95**

Data

Setup

Shot shaping

The post-shot routine

CHAPTER 6 *Practice*   **103**

12-week program for weekend golfer

12-week program for aspiring amateur

12-week program for aspiring tour professional

CHAPTER 7 *Physical Fitness*   **115**

Stretching and warm up

Strength training

Cardiovascular conditioning

Nutrition and diet

Rest

CHAPTER 8 *Choosing a good teacher*   **133**

Where to find a good teacher
Your first lesson
How to be a good student
Is your instructor helping?

CHAPTER 9 *The Right Equipment*   **143**

Important club-fitting terms
Where to have your clubs fitted
The club fitting process

CHAPTER 10 *Framework for Change*   **151**

APPENDIX   **157**

Practice & playing journals
The pin ball game
Glossary of terms

INDEX   **169**

ABOUT THE AUTHOR   **172**

FOREWORD
by Nancy Lopez

I met and got to know Dana Rader when she joined the advisory board of my golf club company several years ago. I had heard of Dana before we started to work together, and everything that people said about her turned out to be true. She's a great teacher, a great person, a great motivator, and an inspiration to so many—purely by being herself. But most importantly, Dana loves the game and wants to help her students enjoy it as much as she does. The game of golf needs as many Dana Raders as it can find.

Dana's teaching philosophy is based on time-tested fundamentals and truths; there are no gimmicks or quick fixes or bandaids. She's always learning and trying to find ways to be a better teacher and communicator. Thousands of students have followed her advice, shot consistently lower scores, and come to enjoy the game even more. I'm glad that she has decided to put her wisdom in a book—any golfer of any standard will benefit from what Dana has to say about golf.

Very quietly, the Dana Rader Golf School has become one of the finest and most respected instructional centers in the country. Julie Cole, the Director of Instruction, played for many years on the LPGA Tour and always had one of the finest short games of any player I have known. Dana, Julie, and the staff at the school are excellent instructors who help a wide variety of players.

As you'll discover in this book, Dana started as an apprentice professional. In 20 years, through hard work and a dedication to being the best that she can be, Dana has become a *GOLF Magazine* Top

100 teacher, a *Golf Digest* Top 50 teacher, and a *Golf for Women* Top 50 teacher, meaning that she is one of the best in the business—male or female. She'll be the first to admit that golf has given a lot to her and she'll be the first to cite her faith as her backbone; she's also the first to give back to the game and to those in need. I found this out when she and I recently worked at a March of Dimes charity clinic.

I also worked with Dana on a video and Dana analyzed my swing for *Golf for Women* magazine. Dana has an excellent grasp of the technical and has a great eye; she can communicate the complex with clarity. That's just part of the reason why she won the LPGA Teacher of the Year Award in 1991. When she critiqued my swing, I realized that she's not a "one-swing-fits-all" teacher; she understands that every golfer is different and adapts to each students' abilities and idiosyncrasies.

Many excellent teaching professionals build their reputations by traveling with the various tours, working in the spotlight with LPGA and PGA stars. Dana, remarkably, has built her reputation at the grass roots level, one golfer at a time. After getting to know Dana and working with her as a fellow professional, I'm convinced that if more golfers followed Dana's philosophies, there would be more fairways and greens hit in regulation, more birdies, more up-and-downs, more single-digit handicappers, and more enjoyment and fun on golf courses all over the United States.

Rock Solid Golf is the type of golf book that every golfer should read. It provides an excellent blueprint and road map for success. The book is based on sound philosophies and reflects Dana's character, experience, and expertise. I'm glad that I met Dana and always look forward to working with her.

It is not good to have zeal without knowledge,
nor to be hasty and miss the way.

PROVERBS 19:2

PREFACE

"How did you become a teacher?"

"Did you ever try to play professionally?"

Sometimes—though no one has ever asked this directly—the underlying question is, "Are you a teacher because you weren't good enough to compete professionally?"

I'm always happy to answer questions about my career path because it's natural for a student to want to know his teacher's credentials. A little knowledge about your instructor's background establishes trust. Of course, it's a superficial trust, but it's a start. What happens in the future—whether or not you improve—is what matters most. But first, let me answer your initial questions.

In 1982, I tried to qualify for the LPGA Tour. This meant going to the finals of "Q-School," which is the annual, weeklong tournament where 144 outstanding golfers battle for 20 guaranteed, full-time spots on the tour for that season. Because there's so much on the line, Q-School is a brutal event. The best of friends ignore each other. Most competitors find it difficult to eat and sleep, let alone hit their best shots.

Like many young golfers who played well in junior and college tournaments, I had dreams of making a living as a professional touring golfer, jetting around the world, competing on the great courses, joking with fellow pros on the practice green, earning healthy paychecks, winning championships, and becoming famous. But at Q-School, the dream became a nightmare.

That year, the tournament took place at Bent Tree Golf & Country Club, a difficult course in Sarasota, Florida. When I arrived for Q-School, my game was a mess. To make matters worse, the weather experts forecast a week of wind, rain, and record-low temperatures. At the players' meeting the day before the tournament, I had this terrible feeling that my name would be selected for an early tee time and, sure enough, when the draw began, the first words spoken by the official in charge of the tournament were:

"From Charlotte, North Carolina—Dana Rader."

My heart sank. I would begin Q-School at 6:50 the next morning. That night, I slept for 10 minutes. When I arrived at the tee at 6:45, there was a frost delay…of nearly three hours! I hit my first shot just before noon. Nervous and exhausted, I played the worst round of my professional career and failed to qualify.

It was a long trip home.

Fortunately, I'd lined up a job as an assistant professional at Myers Park Country Club in Charlotte and had my first lesson as an instructor to return to. It paid $12 an hour, hardly what I'd expected to make as a tour professional, but still seemed princely.

A few days after returning from Sarasota, with the oak trees in full autumnal riot, I started work with my first student, a left-handed beginner. After a few swings, I saw she was picking the club-head off the ground too quickly. She needed to sweep the club back from the ball low.

"Don't pick the club up," I said with an authority that belied my minute of instructional experience. The student stopped and thought for a minute, then posed this question:

"How else am I going to get the club off the ground?"

My first lesson taught me the need for precise communication.

Those early lessons on the tee at Myers Park and my experience at Q-School taught me another lesson: I was meant to teach. To go from near despair to the exhilaration of helping someone in less than a week was a clear signal.

I threw myself into learning everything I could about professional golf instruction. I traveled the country to attend PGA- and LPGA-sponsored "teach-the-teacher" seminars. I studied instruction under excellent teachers like Peggy Kirk Bell at Pine Needles in Southern Pines, North Carolina. Sometimes, I'd find a bench at a driving range and watch the golfers, rehearsing what I might say to them if they were on my lesson tee. I read hundreds of books about golf instruction and teaching.

And, most importantly, I gave lessons. My teaching schedule filled quickly as word got around that a young woman at Myers Park Country Club had a gift for helping people learn and improve.

Though I'm a much better teacher for all the professional instruction I've received from colleagues, I credit my students for teaching me the most. After more than 20,000 hours on the lesson tee, I'm still learning from the men and women who take instruction from me.

When I wake up each morning, I can't wait to get to my school. To me, there's nothing more exhilarating and rewarding than helping a student improve his game. And for all the wisdom I impart to my students, they always manage to teach me a thing or two.

So, am I a teacher because I couldn't make a living as a touring professional? No. I'm a teacher because I love teaching.

As long as I live, I hope I'll be able to continue teaching. And learning.

INTRODUCTION

As I mentioned in the Preface, my experience trying to qualify for the LPGA Tour more than 20 years ago provided me with a number of insights—first and foremost that I was meant to be a teacher. But the Q-School experience taught me several other lessons. Here's the most important.

To play golf consistently well, you must build your game upon the foundation of the correct fundamentals.

When—not *if* but *when*—mental clutter attempts to distract your focus, your rock solid foundation will not shake.

Here's what I mean.

My game leading up to Q-School was not where I wanted it to be. I was worried. In my frustration, I thought it best to seek counsel from several teachers and friends.

"Okay, how should I play the greens if they're fast?" I'd ask. "Should I go for a fade on No. 3 or head straight down the middle?" "My swing seems a little slow for the Tour. What do you think?" "What do you think of my pre-shot routine?"

My questions continued like this for weeks. I received a head full of answers. Imperceptibly, I slipped further and further away from my rock solid fundamentals. By the time I arrived at Q-School, I was possibly the most confused golfer in the field—and it showed. I shot the worst round of my professional life.

I'd forgotten the most important lesson that Joe Cheves— the head professional at Mimosa Hills Golf Club in my hometown of Morganton, North Carolina—taught me in my first golf lesson as a teenager.

"In golf," he said, "there are many more teachers than players." Joe was gently warning me that I'd receive more instruction in life than I could ever use. To improve, I would want to pick one learning model and stick to it. Jumping from model to model, or tip to tip, would confuse me and harm my game.

Here's an interesting fact: Despite measurable and significant improvements in golf ball design, club performance, golf course conditioning, and instruction, the average handicap—according to research conducted by the National Golf Foundation—has changed very little since the early 1980s.

Some of my teaching colleagues believe the reason for this phenomenon is that golfers pay too little attention to the short game. This is true. But another reason is that golfers are confused. Magazines, golf shows on television, friends, and even well-meaning strangers bombard us with suggestions for improvement. Many of the suggestions are sound. But taken out of context as part of a whole model for improvement, they'll disrupt your game.

In this book, you'll find my model for improvement. It's based on the fundamentals of grip, posture, stance, ball position, target alignment, and target awareness. No matter what level of player I work with—from beginner to Tour professional—I check their fundamentals first and insist upon correcting any inefficiencies before we move on. Why?

Proper fundamentals produce consistency in the swing, and consistency is the defining characteristic of every good player.

This model works for busy executives, weekend warriors, aspiring professionals, men, women, girls, boys, right-handers, "lefties," and everyone in between. Of course, I am not the only instructor to stress the fundamentals.

Last year, at a conference in Sacramento, California, I met Butch Harmon, Tiger Woods' coach. At dinner one night, I had the chance to ask about his approach to teaching. I was not surprised to learn that one of the best teachers in the world, when working with the best golfer in the world, stresses and constantly monitors grip, ball position, posture, stance, alignment, and target awareness—the fundamentals. Tiger's foundation is superb. That's a big part of why he is one of the greatest players in the history of the game.

Rock Solid Golf begins with a chapter called "Misconceptions" because 99 percent of students arrive at my lesson tee with preconceived, and often incorrect, notions about how to play the game. Before I can help you build a foundation for your game, we've got to tear down the old ideas that may be hindering your progress. Next, we build the foundation: how to develop and maintain proper grip, posture, stance, alignment, ball position, and target awareness.

From this foundation, we build the swing. With sound fundamentals, you'll be surprised how much easier it is to create a sound swing that consistently creates playable ball flight. The short game, or the scoring game as it's also aptly known, follows. For each short game shot—chips, pitches, bunker shots, and putts—you'll find a description of how the proper use of the fundamentals forms the basis of success. In "The Pre-Shot Routine" chapter, you'll discover how a powerful yet simple process repeated before every shot can guarantee your fundamentals are correct and position you for success each time you hit the ball.

There are practice sections throughout the book following every bit of new instruction, including suggested drills, and there's also an entire chapter devoted to how to develop a specific, 12-week practice regimen for success for three levels of players: weekend golfers, aspiring amateurs, and touring professionals. A chapter on physical fitness provides information and specific suggestions for stretching, cardiovascular workouts, and strength training for this often-overlooked aspect of the game.

Chapter eight, "Choosing A Good Teacher," will aid in your search for someone who can implement the model put forth in this book. Just as I'm not a one-swing-fits-all instructor, I'm also not a one-book-is-all-you-need author. I don't think it's realistic to read a book, take the drills to the course, and assume that you'll be playing superb golf in two days. You'll improve, of course, but the most significant improvement will come when an instructor complements the advice in this book.

The same goes for equipment, and chapter nine explains why custom-fit clubs are important. Finally, in the last chapter, "Framework for Change," you'll see how to put this entire model of improvement together.

If you're one of the millions of golfers who have ceased learning and improving due to information overload, you'll benefit from reading this book. But whether or not this book helps you build a rock solid foundation for your game or becomes just another title in your enormous golf-improvement library is up to you.

If you commit to this model of improvement, you'll get much better. If you read through this book looking for a few good tips or for an easy fix, you won't improve much.

Building a swing based on the fundamentals is not easy. It's never been trendy, and progress is rarely quick. But the method contained on the following pages *does* work. I've seen it happen many, many times and look forward to hearing that it also worked for you. So, let's get started, shall we?

A Note about the Text:

Purely for the sake of brevity,
I have used a right-handed model.

ONE

MISCONCEPTIONS

All learning follows a model, and when someone arrives at my school—unless they've never picked up a club or discussed with another golfer their intention to learn—they show up with a model, or method of thinking, about how to play the game. Before any instruction begins, I want to know about each student's golf thinking. More often than not, I find that their model of learning includes one or more of the game's common misconceptions, such as *Keep your head down*; or *Tuck your right elbow*; or *Don't sway*. Some misconceptions are so prevalent that even non-golfers have been heard to say, "Your head should be perfectly still during the swing." (It shouldn't, but more on that later.)

Each misconception in this chapter contains a kernel of truth and was developed as advice to help golfers correct a common swing ailment, such as the flying elbow or the arms collapsing at the top of the backswing. So what's wrong with this advice, especially if it seems to fix a persistent problem you're having? Well, what appears to be your solution today can quickly become the source of all your problems tomorrow. In other words, the advice that temporarily fixes your flying elbow may kick off a chain reaction of problems that make the flying elbow look like a pleasant problem to have.

Golf is too intricate a game for "one-size-fits-all" advice. What works for a short, stocky player with arms that naturally turn outward, will not necessarily translate well to a tall, lanky player with inward-turning arms. It's only natural to want to believe that a simple tip will provide instant and permanent gratification, but I've yet to find such a magical cure. Lifetime improvement based on sound fundamentals is the goal, and this requires discipline and patience.

That's not easy when advice on how to play better golf comes from your spouse, your doctor, even complete strangers on the golf course. Not surprisingly, many golfers build their portfolio of misconceptions with the help of players who are not professional golf teachers. If a new student tells me that keeping the right elbow tucked is key, I'll ask:

> Golf tips are like aspirin. One may do you good, but if you swallow the whole bottle, you'll be lucky to survive.
>
> HARVEY PENICK

"Who told you that?"

"The guy building my deck," might be the reply.

What follows are some of the game's most pervasive misconceptions. For each, I describe why the misconception exists (what common problem the advice is intended to fix) and what the unintended consequences of following the advice can be. In each case, one of the unintended consequences is an adverse impact on one or more of the ball flight laws, which are the rules of physics as they relate to the impact between the club and the golf ball. (See "The Ball Flight Laws" on page 10.) Finally, for each misconception, I provide a brief description (that's expanded upon in later chapters) of how the proper use of the fundamentals will solve the problem.

After reading this chapter and examining the misconceptions at work in your own game, you'll be ready for the following advice to steer you away from misconceptions forever:

- Listen to your PGA or LPGA teaching professional.
- Politely ignore everyone else.

Misconception: Keep your head down (a.k.a. Don't look up)
Problem it's meant to correct: Topping
Problems it creates: Loss of power, consistency, and momentum; poor posture

If you've ever been told to keep your head down through the swing, someone probably suggested that as a cure for topping the ball. (Topping is when your club glances across the very top of the ball, sending it just a few yards off the tee—it's as close as you can come to missing the ball completely.) Beginners top the ball a lot and often hear "Don't look up" as well-intended advice. Unfortunately, it's poor advice.

> The worst advice in golf is, 'Keep your head down.'
> PATTY SHEEHAN

Here's the problem: Simply looking up does not cause

THE BALL FLIGHT LAWS

Golf is a game open to many levels of interpretation, but one part of the sport is not open to debate: the laws of physics. I stress the fundamentals because they are the best way to make use of physics in your pursuit of playing well. You do not need a degree from M.I.T. to improve at golf, but it helps to have a basic understanding of the forces at work in the game. Dr. Gary Wiren, a noted golf researcher and instructor, worked with the National Golf Foundation to produce the following laws of ball flight.

Path – The club must be on the correct path; this controls direction.

Speed – The club must be traveling with significant speed at impact; this produces distance.

Angle of approach – The club must approach the ball at the correct angle.

Centeredness of the clubface – The club must contact the ball in the sweet spot.

Squareness of the clubface – The club must be square with the target at impact.

Consider these laws to be just that: LAWS. If you're going to strike the ball correctly, your swing must comply with the five laws of ball flight. They represent the marriage of the fundamentals with physics. With excellent fundamentals, you can create the right swing path, generate the correct speed from the ideal angle of approach, and make contact with the ball in the center of a squared club.

So, when you hit a perfect shot, you can now turn to your partners and explain, using the laws of physics, why the ball landed a few feet from the flag and stopped right next to the hole.

topping. Instead, poor posture and/or incorrect ball position are the most likely culprits, both of which create problems in your swing plane. The beginner trying to keep her head down has to make erratic adjustments in her swing to hit the ball square, and if she continues playing without correcting the fundamentals—posture and ball position, for example—she'll never develop consistency in her game.

What happens when you keep your head down through the swing? First, you lose the following:

rotation

balance, as you rock on your heels or toes

momentum

power

consistency

Keeping your head down skews the **angle of approach** and slows the **speed** of the clubhead at impact, two of the vital ball flight laws governing how straight and far the ball travels. Finally, keeping your head down puts too much emphasis on the ball, rather than on the correct movement of the swing. As you'll see in the chapter on the pre-shot routine, the best way to keep the mind clear during your game is to develop one thought about your swing— *smooth takeaway* or *swing through*, for example—and focus all your attention on that one thought.

"But what about the pros?" an inquisitive student will ask, showing me a picture of Tiger Woods looking at the ball at impact as proof.

These pictures present a split second of the swing and fail to capture the follow through, where the head rises. If you watch slow-motion replays of the superb swings of Annika Sorenstam or David Duval, you'll see that neither is looking at the ball at impact. Their heads are already turning toward the target with the powerful momentum of their swings.

What's the solution for topping? The most likely fix will involve correcting your posture or ball position, but it might also involve re-sizing your clubs or practicing your swing daily for several weeks to develop proper rhythm. We'll get to all of those issues later in the book. For now what I want you to know is that keeping your head down is great advice for taking an exam in school and bad advice for the golf swing.

Misconception: Keep the right elbow tucked
Problem it's meant to correct: Loss of distance; a slice
Problems it creates: Lack of width in the swing causing loss of power and speed

The tip, "Keep your right elbow tucked," is intended to fix a "flying elbow," which is when the back arm—that's the right arm for right-handed golfers—rises quickly in the backswing and "flies" above the shoulders. It looks like a raised chicken wing. A flying elbow produces any number of problems, including slices, shanks, or drives that land well short of the intended target.

Hit a slice and a well-meaning bystander will suggest: "Keep your right elbow tucked at address and through the top of the back-swing." A few practice swings with the right elbow tucked produce what *feels* like extra power, but what's really happening is your hands and the right forearm come too close to the right shoulder and end up collapsed (rather than having the left arm comfortably extended). As a result, you reduce the width of your swing plane, resulting in less speed, power, and distance. The ball flight laws adversely affected include the **path** of the clubface, **angle of approach**, and **speed** of the clubface.

If you try to throw a golf ball with the elbow of your throwing arm tucked close to your ribs, it's difficult. You'll feel like a shot putter, and chances are you won't throw a Calloway much farther than an Olympian throws a 16-pound iron ball. It's easier to throw with the elbow extended away from

> **Apply your heart to instruction and your ears to words of knowledge.**
> PROVERBS 23:12

the body. The same dynamics apply to your backswing. Check out photos of most professional golfers with excellent backswings and you'll see that their right elbows are not tucked at the top of the swing but are extended away from their torsos.

So if you're slicing, shanking, or your drives are falling short because of a flying elbow or a collapsed backswing, how should you fix it? The answer lies, of course, in correcting your fundamentals. The most likely culprits are poor posture and/or a poor grip, resulting in a poor shoulder turn and, thus, a swing that's off plane. The next chapter about the fundamentals will help you avoid problems in your swing plane.

What's important to know now is this: Tucking your elbow will not cure slicing or shanking, and it certainly won't help you generate power. Power comes from a good setup, solid contact between the club and ball with the clubface square to the target, a good shoulder turn, and good timing. We'll get to those shortly.

Misconception: Keep the left arm straight or stiff
Problem it's meant to correct: A collapsing left arm at the top of the backswing
Problems it creates: Tension in the swing; less power and distance; increased chance of injury

If your left arm bends, or collapses, at the top of the back-swing, you're bound to hear the following advice: "Keep your left arm straight and stiff." Why? A collapsed left arm creates many problems, including slicing, lack of power, poor accuracy, inconsistency, and the list goes on. But the answer is not to correct the problem by keeping your left arm ramrod straight.

When you follow this misconception, you create tension in your swing, and *nothing* kills a good swing like tension. Keeping your left arm rigid through the swing shortens your swing, adversely affecting the ball flight laws of the *angle of approach, speed,* and *path* of the clubface. That means you end up with less power and distance.

In spite of these drawbacks, there are still instructors who teach students to play with a stiff left arm. Some even suggest students correct a collapsed left arm by imagining their arm encased in a cast. Ouch! Keeping your left arm stiff through the swing hurts, and you run a greater chance of injury, including tendonitis and soreness in your arm and shoulders.

So how should your left arm position itself through the swing? Look at the photo of my swing on page 49 and you'll see that my left arm is comfortably extended at the top of my backswing. From this position, I can generate tremendous power. But to be honest, I

A PAINFUL LESSON

When I was preparing to attend Q-School, the rigorous proving grounds where aspiring LPGA players compete against one another for spots on the Tour, I visited an instructor who noticed I was losing width at the top of the swing. His suggestion? Keep my left arm rigid. Eager to find the fix that would send me on to the Big Show, I swung with a stiff left arm for 30 minutes, even though my mind was thinking: "This is uncomfortable and painful." That half-hour practice had a lingering side effect: a painful case of tendonitis that kept me from playing for several weeks. Some time later—after I chose teaching over a career as a professional player—I learned that what I really needed that day was advice on how to make a better pivot. Instead, I fell victim to a misconception and learned first hand how many problems a misconception can create!

never ask students to think about their left arms. Instead, I focus on helping them create a good pivot, which creates a swing driven by the large muscles of the shoulders. A good pivot naturally produces a position at the top of the backswing with the left arm comfortably extended. Let's leave the stiff left arm where it belongs—on the Heisman Trophy.

Misconception: Don't sway; Keep your head still
Problem it's meant to correct: Inconsistency; hooking the ball; pushing the ball to the right of the target
Problems it creates: A reverse pivot; tension in the swing; loss of balance; inconsistency

Just as you'd imagine, "Don't sway" is intended to correct what looks like a dance move—when your body sways laterally to the right during the backswing. A golfer who sways on the back-swing must also sway on the downswing, and this movement produces inconsistency. The more lateral movement in your golf swing, the less likely you are to hit the ball square with the clubface.

Another variation on the same advice is "Keep your head still," since lateral movement by the body also makes the head move forward and back. But if swaying is bad in the swing, then what's wrong with the advice, "Don't sway," or "Keep your head still?"

First, whenever you're told not to move, the first thing you do is tense up and freeze, and as I just mentioned, nothing kills a golf swing like tension. Golf is about movement, but it's a circular movement rather than excessive side-to-side motion. If you concentrate on keeping your head still, you'll forget about the circular movement the shoulders must make for a good swing. And that's just the beginning of the negative consequences brought about by keeping your head still.

Because the head is one of the heaviest parts of the body—it weighs about 15 pounds—trying to keep it still is very difficult and will throw off your balance. If your head stays over or even in front of the ball during the takeaway to the top of the backswing, your weight is on the forward foot. Then, your weight shifts to the back foot as you swing through. This is called a reverse pivot (see page 59) and is the opposite of how your weight should move during the swing. The reverse pivot produces just about every kind of undesirable shot the game has to offer: hooks, slices, pushes, pulls, fat shots, thin shots, complete misses, and everything in between. In fact, the only consistent result of a reverse pivot is inconsistency.

The ball flight laws compromised by following this misconception include the *angle of approach*, *speed*, and *path* of the clubface.

Where should the head be during the swing? The left side of your face should be behind the ball at all times, and it's fine to move your head backward a few inches from the ball during the swing. But I'd rather you not focus on head position at all during the swing. Instead, I want you to think about your shoulder turn.

To correct a golfer who sways or one with a reverse pivot, I work to help her make a better shoulder turn. Note that I'm suggesting a *better* turn, not a *bigger* shoulder turn. (A huge turn is not necessary to generate power and can actually decrease power when too big of a turn puts you in an awkward position where you have to fight the club.) A good shoulder turn is the result of setting up with the right grip, posture, stance, ball position, and target awareness. When you make a good turn, you'll avoid excess lateral movement (or sway), and the weight will be on the back foot at the top of the backswing—where it should be.

To create a good shoulder turn it helps to know where your hands and arms are supposed to be during the swing, and I cover that in the chapter on the swing. For now, I want your hands and arms holding this book and continuing to turn the pages.

Misconception: Play the ball off the forward foot
Problem it's meant to correct: Poor ball position
Problems it creates: Inconsistency; poor posture
and alignment

If someone suggests you play the ball off the forward foot, they're most likely reacting to your placing the ball either too far

FREEZE FRAME

Some of the staunchest defenders of the "Keep your head still" misconception include golfers who've read Jack Nicklaus' best-selling book *Golf My Way*, in which he talks about keeping the head absolutely still during the swing. I'm a big fan of the Golden Bear, but I disagree with that piece of advice. First of all, it's impossible to keep your head perfectly still! Your head, thanks to your neck, is connected to your shoulders, and your shoulders are supposed to turn during the swing. In fact, if you look at sequential photos of Nicklaus' swing—or view it on video frame-by-frame with a box drawn around his head—you'll see that his head moves some two to three inches behind the ball during the backswing.

forward or too far back in your stance. Sometime in the history of golf, someone came up with playing the ball off the forward foot as one-position-fits-all advice. But, as we've already learned, golf is not a game that lends itself to universal rules.

Where should the ball be in the stance? That's easy. When the club gets to impact, the ball had better be there! Seriously, if every shot with every club is played inside the left heel, awkward compensations must be made to generate power and get the club square at impact. Those compensations will wreak havoc on your swing plane, decreasing the chances that you'll make optimal use of the ball flight laws. Specifically, you'll be unlikely to generate the proper clubhead *speed* or have your clubface *square* to the ball at impact.

> It took me 17 years to get 3,000 hits in baseball. I did it in one afternoon on the golf course.
>
> HANK AARON

Ball position is a fundamental covered in detail in the following chapter, but the general rules governing where the ball should be in your stance depend upon the club you're using, the terrain, and the ball's lie.

Misconceptions about the takeaway

Ah yes, the takeaway. If someone could wave a magic wand and dispel all the misconceptions built around the backswing, golf scores would drop dramatically. Granted, the takeaway sets up the success or failure of the swing, and it's challenging to get right because your body must turn on two planes—your arms on one, your shoulders on another—but the only sure-fire way to make it really difficult is to fall victim to one or more of the takeaway misconceptions.

Even though the three major misconceptions—"Cock the wrists," "Take the club straight back with the toe up," and "Take it back low and slow"—are intended to correct different problems with the takeaway, I address them together because they share the same solution. For the most part, they're also caused by the same error—lack of attachment to the target. If you begin your takeaway without a target in mind, you're heading for trouble in your swing. The *right* way to fix trouble in the takeaway is through—surprise!—mastery of the fundamentals, especially alignment, target awareness, grip, and posture.

"Cock the wrists" is common advice given to golfers who make poor contact with the ball and/or lack power. The fundamental flaw behind this advice is the belief that the wrists create power in the swing. (Power comes from the shoulders and hips rather than the arms and wrists.) When you think about cocking, or setting, your wrists, you end up with excessive hands action, forcing the forearms to over-rotate on the backswing.

Perfect hand position and wrist-set during the swing come from the correct setup. The fundamentals of grip and posture (for grip, see page 25, and for posture, page 30) facilitate a good turn, and with a good turn, the hands hinge naturally to produce all the wrist set you'll ever need.

Golfers with poor backswings often hear they need to work on getting more width or extension in their takeaway. That's usually true. Unfortunately, the common advice for this—*"Take the club straight back,"* or *"Keep the toe up"*—leads the player to over-think the takeaway, which typically results in getting off plane at the top of the backswing. If you're off plane in the backswing, the only way to hit the ball square is to make adjustments during the downswing. Making those corrections consistently in your swing is nearly impossible. You're much better off developing a swing that's on plane during the entire backswing. Start with the correct posture, stance, grip, and alignment, whereby your hands, arms, and shoulders will naturally stay connected in the backswing. This produces enough extension to generate significant power in the swing—without having to think about extension or width.

The last, and perhaps most common, misconception about the takeaway is to *"Take the club back low and slow."* The advice is meant to correct an extremely quick or steep backswing. When a golfer hears this advice, he is apt to take the club back *too* low and *too* slowly. Take the club back too low and the shoulders dip, which creates any number of problems, including fat shots—where the club hits the ground before hitting the ball, leaving a large divot. Take it back too slowly and you must generate power by rushing at the top of the backswing, which creates a jerky move from the top down and typically results in a slice.

The ideal swing is connected and evenly paced, but if a student's natural inclination is to swing quickly, I won't necessarily change his tempo. Instead, I'll work to make sure his shoulders turn properly and his backswing remains on plane. The trick is to focus on the correct setup, rather than on the speed of the swing. Your natural pace will develop through the right use of the fundamentals. After all, Billy Joe Patton—the great amateur from my hometown of Morganton, North Carolina, who almost won the Masters in 1953—had a backswing that was a blur. And Nancy Lopez, one of the world's greatest golfers, has a backswing that's nice and slow.

Are the misconceptions in this chapter the only ones you'll run into as you continue to play golf? Or course not! An entire book could be written about common but incorrect advice on how to improve your game. These are just the most persistent misconceptions I run across daily in my career as a teaching professional. Chances are, you've heard—or spread—a few of these yourself.

If any of these are part of the model by which you've learned to play golf, it's time to forget them. We're going to start with a clean slate, and I'm going to

> ## The Lord answers my prayers everywhere except on the golf course.
> **REV. BILLY GRAHAM**

help you re-build your golf game beginning with a foundation based on the fundamentals.

It's time to get better at golf.

TWO

THE FUNDAMENTALS

If you want to hit drives routinely down the middle of the fairway, your fundamentals must be excellent. If you want to chip superbly and be a wizard out of the sand, your fundamentals must be excellent. If you want to be the best putter at your club, your fundamentals must be excellent. If you want to shoot low scores at legendary and challenging courses like Pinehurst #2 or Pebble Beach or St. Andrews...you guessed it, your fundamentals must be excellent.

Excellent fundamentals create consistency, and consistency is the defining characteristic of every fine player.

So why is it, then, that most golfers who pick up an instruction book avoid the chapter on the fundamentals? Or that players arriving for a lesson grow frustrated if the instructor suggests revisiting the building blocks of the game? Because they think that since they already know the game fairly well, they must have their fundamentals down. Despite all the improvements in technology, the average handicap has not decreased significantly in the past 20 years because the overwhelming majority of golfers pay too little attention to their fundamentals.

> Learn the fundamentals of the game and stick to them. Band-Aid remedies never last.
>
> JACK NICKLAUS

At the beginning of every lesson with every student—whether it's with a beginner, an accomplished amateur, or a professional—I check the key fundamentals:

Grip

Posture & Stance

Ball Position

Alignment & Target Awareness

Getting the fundamentals right without instruction from a book or an instructor is challenging because the natural tendency is to gravitate to what feels *comfortable*, which is usually not the correct form. For example, the best posture for the golf swing is not

A POWERFUL THOUGHT

Just how powerful are the fundamentals? If you've ever witnessed a slender or short golfer consistently out-driving a powerfully built lineman and wondered how that could happen, the answer may lie in the fundamentals. You maximize the chance of nailing the ball *just right* by using a perfect setup. The setup puts you in position to comply with the **ball flight laws** on page 10, the rules governing how straight and far your shot travels. Each of the fundamentals—grip, posture, stance, ball position, alignment, and target awareness—affects all five laws of ball flight.

what feels natural but instead a stance that may feel awkward. The same may be true for the grip. The good news is that practicing the proper fundamentals makes them feel comfortable and natural. With a little time, you'll find reverting to your original, natural tendency is what feels awkward.

In spite of the initial "break-in" period, developing excellent fundamentals is not difficult because no movement is involved. You just have to learn the correct positions, and then you can practice them anywhere.

GRIP

Of all the fundamentals, the grip is the most important because it influences every aspect of the golf swing and has the most impact on the five ball flight laws. The grip is the cornerstone of consistency.

If you arrive at my lesson tee with a bad grip, I'll change it. That's never easy because a grip change is sure to produce a period of readjustment (and awful shots). Some golf teachers try to fit a student's swing around a bad grip, rather than fix the fundamental error. (They're most likely afraid the student will never visit them again.) That's a short-term solution, and it won't provide consistency over the long run.

If you're in the middle of a grip change, understand it will feel unnatural for a while, perhaps even uncomfortable. But practice holding and swinging the club with the new grip and you'll pass through the readjustment quickly. Soon your drives will fly

> **Good golf begins with a good grip.**
> BEN HOGAN

25

FIX THAT GRIP

When working with a player who's going through the readjustment period of a grip change (i.e. her shots are flying everywhere), I love to share my own grip-change experience as a student under Bob Toski, the former PGA Tour star and well-known instructor.

When I was 19, in college, and feeling pretty good about my game, I thought a lesson from a top teacher would help me get to the professional level as a player. One spring break, I drove to Fort Lauderdale—not to party—but to take a lesson from Bob Toski. He took one look at my grip and said:

"With that grip, you'll never play professional golf."

He gave me a choice: "Fix that grip or get off my tee." I stayed. It took time to adjust to what felt like a radically new grip, and I felt discouraged when my drives fell from 250 yards to 210. But Mr. Toski turned out to be right. My old grip wouldn't hold up under pressure. With the old grip, I had to make difficult compensations in my swing for various shots, especially finesse and pitch shots around the green, and those adjustments cost me consistency.

Over time, I regained my distance and then some. More importantly, my swing was built upon a rock solid fundamental, and the result soon showed where I most wanted it, on the scorecard!

farther with a better, more consistent ball flight. Your swing will hold up under pressure and in difficult weather. But until you reach that point, you'll have to take my word for it. I've changed the grips of hundreds of students. A few left me because the results were so awful—initially. But many more believed they would get a lot better...and did. A grip change requires patience.

Types of Grip

I recommend one of two grips to students—the overlap or the interlocking—and the recommendation typically depends on the size of the player's hands. Both of the grips keep the hands united through the swing and allow the hands to hinge properly.

The *overlap grip* is best for golfers with average- or large-sized hands. To grip the club properly, lay the handle of the club across the base of the fingers of the left hand. Rotate

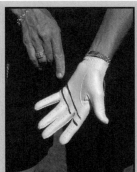

The lines on this glove show where the grip should be placed in the left hand.

Grip the club at the base of the fingers, not in the palm.

The "V" between the forefinger and thumb should point to the right shoulder.

The right hand "V" should also point to the right shoulder.

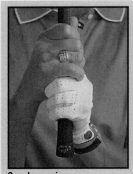

Overlap grip.   Interlocking grip.

the hand to the right to where you see two knuckles. (If you see one or three knuckles, rotate your hand to a position where you see only two.)

Place the right hand on the club, below the left hand, placing it in the middle of the fingers. Place the lifeline of the right hand, which is next to the pad of the thumb, over the left hand thumb. Ideally, there should be a "V" between the thumb and forefinger on each hand. Each "V" should point to a spot between the chin and the right shoulder.

In the overlap grip, the right pinkie lies between the middle and forefinger of the

> If a golfer doesn't have a good grip, he has two chances: slim and none.
> GENE SARAZEN

left hand. You create the *interlocking grip* the same way except the pinkie on the right hand interlocks between the middle and forefinger of the left hand. The interlocking grip is typically better for golfers with smaller hands.

Common Grip Errors

A common problem I run across is what I call the "Honda grip," which is where the left hand is rotated too far on top of the club to where you can see four or five knuckles. Other instructors may call this an overly *strong grip*. To me, it looks like the player is gripping the handlebars of a motorcycle. A golfer with a Honda grip can sometimes hit the ball a mile but tends to hook the ball or scoop it off the ground.

Another grip error I see often is the **weak grip**, where either one or no

A weak grip.   A strong grip.

knuckles of the left hand can be seen, and the "V" points to the left shoulder. With this grip, it's difficult to square the clubface and shots tend to fly to the right.

To correct an overly strong or weak grip, rebuild your grip according to the directions above.

A QUICK GRIP TIP

A common grip error is to place the club in the palm. Your grip should begin in the base of the fingers and *not* in the palm. Here's a quick way to check your grip: Examine your golf glove. If there's a lot of wear—a hole or tear—in the heel of the glove, you're looking at the evidence for why you tend to slice the ball or hit weakly to the right. If you're properly gripping the club, you won't find a hole or tear above the heel path of the glove.

Pressure is a key component of a good grip, and while some golfers hold the club too loosely in the fingers, most hold it with far too much pressure. If you are gripping the club so tightly that I couldn't easily pull it out of your hands, then you need to relax your grip pressure.

To determine the proper grip pressure, grip

> ## A golfer who stands at the ball as rigid as a statue usually becomes a monumental failure.
>
> ### DICK AULTMAN

the club and hold it upright, perpendicular to the ground. Loosen your hold until it feels as if the club is just about to slip through your fingers. This is the pressure you want.

POSTURE & STANCE

Posture is simply a way of saying, "Here's how to stand at address." Good posture facilitates an athletic swing powered by the large muscles of the shoulders. You'll read more in "The Swing" chapter about how a good pivot powered by a shoulder turn provides consistent punch in the swing. To harness all your power, your posture must be correct at address.

Here's the correct posture—from the ground up—beginning with the stance.

Match your feet width to the widest part of your body, either your hips or shoulders. If the feet are too far apart at address, your swing may become too flat, which results in reduced power. If the feet are too close at address, you'll be off balance when you turn.

A FOOTNOTE

Golfers with hip, knee, or feet problems may find it difficult or painful to keep the back foot square. Try this: Point your back foot out a little to alleviate any pain. I've had success with this after my knee surgery. Pointing the back foot out slightly helps me move my weight better on the backswing.

A straight back bent from the hips to a 45-degree angle.

Perfect posture looks athletic.

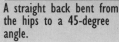

With the proper stance, your swing will be in balance and you can generate power from a good shoulder turn. The front foot should be a little open with the toes pointing out slightly while the back foot should be square, or perpendicular, to the target line. This makes it easier to place the ball in the right position at address.

The knees should be slightly flexed with hips and fanny out. The back should be straight and tilted at 45 degrees, and you should bend at the hips *not at the waist*. No slouching or standing up too straight. The shoulders should be over the middle part of the shoes, with the arms hanging straight down from the shoulders. This will place your hands directly under your chin. I like to see the chin up, not glued to the base of the neck. This posture will place you the correct distance from the ball.

You could use this position to guard someone in basketball, play shortstop in baseball, or block someone in football. Good golf posture looks athletic, yet someone who isn't athletic can easily develop good posture when they address the ball.

The best way to maintain good posture—once you've developed it on the lesson tee—is to practice it in front of a mirror to receive crucial, visual feedback. Of course, if you spend too much time in front of the mirror, you'll get a different kind of feedback—from your spouse or roommate.

Even after playing golf with correct posture for years, maintaining it requires vigilance. Deterioration usually begins with the chin dropping toward the chest. Another danger inherent in the misconception, "Keep the head down," is that it can push the chin down to your chest, making it very difficult to achieve a good pivot. When I tell students to keep their chin up, some reply that they're worried about not being able to see the ball at address. In the correct posture, you'll be able to see the ball with your chin up.

SOME INSIGHTFUL ADVICE

Golfers who have to wear bifocals or trifocals are often forced to tuck their chin just to see the ball. To make matters worse, their bifocals tend to distort depth perception, creating fat shots and making shots off uneven lies very difficult. I recommend you find an optometrist—preferably one who plays golf or has corrected this problem for golfers—and get his help selecting a pair of glasses that minimizes these hindrances.

Changing your posture feels awkward. You'll tire easily as you start using underutilized muscles, and your body will beg to return to slouching. Don't. Good posture is essential to playing well, and you'll want to stay the course as you improve your stance. The best way to pass through this period quickly is to head to the gym for some weight training. In the chapter on physical fitness (page 115), you'll find recommended strength training for the back, shoulder, and abdominal muscles, all of which need to be strong for good posture.

BALL POSITION

So your grip and posture are perfect. Where should the ball be in the stance at address? In the last chapter, I discussed the misconception that the ball should be placed just inside the forward foot for

> **Poor ball position is a silent killer.**
> TIGER WOODS

all clubs. Ball position depends on the length of the club. Here are the four basic ball positions:

1. *In the middle of the stance* for wedges and short irons up to a 7-iron

2. *One ball forward of the middle of the stance* for mid and long irons (from a 6-iron to a 1-iron)

3. *Two balls forward of the middle of the stance* for fairway woods

4. *Just inside the forward foot* for the driver

I'm not talking about vast differences in position. Ball position is a subtle art with powerful consequences—just an inch forward or back makes a huge difference in how solidly you hit the ball.

In addition to grip and posture, ball position affects where your hands are at address. If these three fundamentals are correct, your hands will automatically be in the right place at address. An incorrect ball position forces the hands too far

Ball positions begin in the center and move forward as the clubs get longer.

ahead or behind the ball, preventing the arms from fully extending, and creating topped or fat shots.

Sometimes, a good player who is struggling to hit a fairway wood or a wedge will arrive at my lesson tee full of fear that something is drastically wrong with his swing. Imagine his pleasure when he learns it was just ball position.

ALIGNMENT & TARGET AWARENESS

Alignment is simply placing your body in position to aim toward the target. However simple it sounds, this is often the most difficult part of the setup because the target can be far off and is not always visible, thus requiring you to select mini-targets for each shot. What's more, many variables—the wind, hazards, or your own alignment tendencies, for example—affect the ball's flight toward the target, thus impacting alignment.

Alignment: the line along the club-head points to the target; the feet are parallel to the target line.

If only lining up correctly were as easy in golf as it is in other sports. A baseball pitcher has the luxury of staring at the catcher's mitt while he's winding up and pitching, and a basketball player shooting a free throw keeps his eyes on the back of the rim. The golfer, on the other hand, takes a brief look at the target at the beginning of the swing but is not looking at the target *during* the swing. So, even if the hole is just 40 yards away, lining up correctly is crucial.

In spite of its importance and the

dangers of poor alignment—pulled shots, slices, and astronomical scores among them—too few golfers pay attention to *where they are aimed.*

> ## Golfers look at the ball and glance at the target. You should look at the target and glance at the ball.
> ### HARVEY PENICK

The first step in alignment is to select a target. Most golfers at the practice range fail to align themselves to a target. For every shot, whether on the course or at the range, select a specific target rather than "the middle of the range" or "somewhere left of the 200-yard marker." For example, instead of stating a target as the middle of the fairway, I'll pick something more defined like the left hand side of a bedroom window on a house behind the green. At the practice range, the target can be the flag that marks 100 yards or 150 yards, or it can be a fence post at the end of the range.

Once you've selected your target, the best way to initiate good alignment is to approach your ball from the side while looking at the target. Then set up to hit the shot. Now comes the moment of truth. To find out if you're

THE GAMES THEY PLAY

Golf course architects are a mischievous breed and enjoy playing tricks on the golfing public by building tee boxes that line up with trees, swamps, houses, and other hazards. Complaining to the American Society of Golf Course Architects is of little use. If the tee box points out-of-bounds, then the tee box points out-of-bounds. Practice aligning to several different targets when you're at the range and you'll soon out-smart even the most cunning golf course architects.

35

aligned to the target, lay your club behind your heels. Where is the club pointing? Where you are actually aimed may surprise you.

As you use this technique, you'll become aware of your alignment tendencies and be able to correct them in your setup. For example, by checking my alignment every practice session, I catch myself aligning to the right of the target, which creates a pull. Aware of the tendency, I can make the small correction to get back on target.

Visit the practice range at a professional golf tournament and you'll see many players asking their caddies to check their alignment to the target with a club or other alignment device.

> **Keep hitting it straight until the wee ball goes in the hole.**
> JAMES BRAID

Getting good at alignment and target awareness takes practice, and the practice is as simple as aligning yourself to many different targets and checking alignment each time. I like to see players make alignment and target awareness practice part of their standard, pre-round warm-up. If you lose accuracy in the middle of a round, check your alignment.

Alignment is related to ball position: If you adjust your alignment when you're about to swing, ball position changes. If you think you are lined up incorrectly as you are about to swing, move away from the ball and re-start your pre-shot routine.

So, there you have it: the fundamentals of golf and the foundation for a rock solid game. Each fundamental affects the five laws of ball flight, affecting the direction and distance the ball travels. Let's quickly review the key points of each.

> There are no born golfers. Some have more natural ability than others, but they've all been made.
>
> BEN HOGAN

Grip – Place the club more in the fingers than the palm. Grip controls the clubface, determining distance and direction.

Posture & Stance – Place your feet shoulder- or hip-width (whichever is wider) apart. Bend from the hips to a 45-degree angle, with a straight back and your fanny out. Posture controls the swing plane, affecting distance and direction.

Ball position – Start in the center and move forward to the inside left heel as the club gets longer. Controls distance and direction.

Alignment & Target Awareness – Align your body parallel to the target. Controls direction.

How good are your fundamentals? If you answer this with anything other than "excellent," or "the best they've ever been," or "as good as the best," you're unlikely to improve your game and become consistent. If you're an experienced player and your game is off,

> Work on the fundamentals constantly.
>
> NICK PRICE

check your fundamentals first. If you're just beginning the game, learn the fundamentals and make them the foundation of your game.

With your fundamentals in place, you're now ready to learn about the swing.

THREE

THE SWING

From the beginning of golf, countless players have searched for it. For centuries, men and women have prayed for it. Hundreds of books and magazine articles have been written about it. And thousands of products promise to help you achieve it. All this for something that doesn't even exist! I'm talking, of course, about *the perfect golf swing.*

While the perfect golf swing is a myth, what's very real, and worth pursuing, is *the right swing for you.* Provided you don't set yourself up for disappointment by expecting perfection, learning about and improving your golf swing is a rewarding journey that's enormous fun. Sure, it's challenging. But what worthwhile isn't?

While most of my students benefit by building their swing around the positions necessary to strike the ball consistently on line, I do not teach a "one-size-fits-all" model. There are enough good golfers with wild backswings who consistently bring their clubheads back into position at impact to prove that rigid swing rules won't work. That's not to say such a player wouldn't benefit from improving her backswing. She probably would. But if her ball flight is consistently playable, who can argue with that? In this chapter, you'll learn the swing model I developed on the lesson tee with hundreds of students, each of whom improved when they stuck to the plan.

> There are no absolutes in golf. Golf is such an individual game, and no two people swing alike.
> KATHY WHITWORTH

Before we get started, let me stress the importance of reading this chapter in its proper order. If you've opened my book and turned immediately here to diagnose what ails your swing, I hope you'll reconsider and, at least, begin with the previous chapter on the fundamentals. This chapter clarifies the swing. It will help you swing on plane. But without a rock solid foundation built from the game's fundamentals, your swing improvements will be hindered at best.

THE SWING PLANE

The swing is a complicated motion made difficult because your arms, shoulders, and hips all turn on separate planes. Explaining how these different rotations should come together to produce a solid golf swing isn't easy. In fact, it's difficult. During the course of my career, I've found that the simplest way to explain the swing to my students is to talk about the swing plane and how swinging "on plane" produces playable ball flight.

Ben Hogan popularized the swing plane concept in 1957

with his groundbreaking book, *Five Lessons: The Modern Fundamentals of Golf* (Simon & Schuster). Many fine instructors have expanded on Hogan's discussion since the book's publication. Simply put, the swing plane is the path your clubhead travels during the swing. The *correct* swing plane, on the other hand, is the ideal path your clubhead *should* travel in order to impact the ball in the center of a squared club.

> ## The ultimate judge of your swing is the flight of the ball.
> ### BEN HOGAN

When someone refers to swinging "on plane," she's saying that the clubhead traveled along the correct swing path to produce playable ball flight.

What does it take to swing on plane? I like to say it takes *getting in the Zone!*

THE PLAYING ZONE

To understand how the swing plane should be shaped, it helps to have a good mental image. Look at the series of pictures on page 43 showing my swing sequence. In the first picture, I am in the proper setup with excellent posture. I've drawn two lines over the photograph. The first line extends from the ball up the shaft of my club through my hips. The second line extends from the ball up through my right shoulder. The space between these two lines is **the Playing Zone**.

Keeping your club in this zone during the backswing and through the downswing to impact will produce playable ball flight.

As my swing progresses, note how the clubhead stays primarily within this zone throughout the swing. If you watch Tour players on TV, you can imagine the same lines drawn over the screen and you'll see that most professional swings stay within the Zone.

But here's the rub: Without video equipment or a mirror, you cannot see whether or not you're swinging inside the Playing Zone. And without a great deal of practice, you certainly cannot feel when you're within the Zone. So how will you know? *When you're consistently producing playable ball flights, you'll know you're in the Zone.*

Is it possible to revamp an off-plane swing and get it into the Playing Zone without instruction or without the visual validation of a mirror or of video equipment? Perhaps. But I'm certain it's considerably more difficult. Here, then, is a fail-safe, four-step process to get into and stay in the Zone.

1. Understand the importance of the fundamentals in building consistency in your swing.

2. Clear your mind of clutter about the swing. Use this chapter to re-program your thoughts.

3. Use a mirror or video to create a swing within the Zone. Then, take the *feel* of swinging inside the Zone and practice it like you've never practiced anything before.

4. Simplify everything you know about your swing into an easy, effective swing thought that helps you create reproducible results.

THE PLAYING ZONE

ARE YOU IN THE ZONE?

Here's a test to determine if your swing falls within the Playing Zone. Take a 5-iron and stand with your back against a wall. Step two feet away from the wall and assume the proper posture at address. Start the club back and swing through your entire swing in slow motion. If you're inside the Zone, your clubhead will come close to the wall but not touch it. Note your hand position at the top of the backswing. If your hands match the height of your right shoulder, you're golden and your wall is safe. If your hands fall above or below the right shoulder, you're outside the Zone. This is also a good test to insure you're not rolling your wrists at takeaway. Rolling the wrists not only puts the club outside the Zone, it's bad news for your wall.

ELEMENTS OF THE SWING

QUICK FACT

A swing path within the Playing Zone produces playable ball flight.

The remaining information in this chapter divides the swing into parts—the takeaway, the middle of the backswing, the top of the backswing, the downswing, impact, and the follow through—because understanding the correct movement at each stage is helpful. Few things, however, are more debilitating to a golfer's swing than thinking about the separate parts while swinging. *The goal in this chapter is to develop a cohesive, smooth swing within the Playing Zone.*

The takeaway

I spend more time teaching the takeaway than any another element of the swing because a correct takeaway is the crucial first step to swinging inside the Zone. An incorrect takeaway forces a golfer to fight the club throughout the swing in order to get the clubface square at impact. Put another way, an incorrect takeaway puts you in trouble before you've barely begun.

With good posture at address, your shoulders, arms, hands, and club form an inverted triangle—isosceles triangle, to be exact—as you can see in the picture to the right. The first step in getting into the Zone is to perform the takeaway *with the triangle intact throughout the motion.* The one-piece takeaway prevents a common error at this early stage of the swing—that of folding or tucking the right elbow too close to the side. (As you'll recall from chapter one, "Misconceptions," tucking your right elbow reduces width in your swing, resulting in less speed, power, and distance. In addition, tucking your elbow causes the arms to separate and sends the club off plane.)

At address, the shoulders, arms, hands, and club form an inverted triangle.

How do you start the first movement back in the takeaway? With your shoulders! That's the best way to keep the triangle intact. Moreover, if you break the triangle by starting the movement with your hands and keeping your shoulders in place, you'll

The correct one-piece takeaway.

lose width and extension in your swing. Width is a key component in generating power. Another way to think of this takeaway error is *if you're snatching your hands away at takeaway, you're breaking the triangle and losing width and extension.*

So here you are, at address. Your arms should feel as if they're lightly adhered to

THE KISS OF DEATH

Rolling the wrists during the takeaway is so detrimental to the swing that I call this action *the kiss of death*. A wrist roll puts the hands and the clubface in opposite positions from where you want them—the hands end up outside the feet while the clubface is positioned behind the back. Put another way, the hands fall over the top line of the Playing Zone and the clubface falls below the bottom line. Correcting this in the remaining 1.7 seconds of your swing calls for a series of uncomfortable moves. It's much easier to get the takeaway correct—without rolling your wrists!

Rolling the wrists at takeaway.

PRACTICE

Because the takeaway gets everything started, I recommend isolating this motion with a practice drill. The **belt-buckle drill** enforces the first crucial element of every successful swing: the one-piece takeaway. Get in the correct posture at address and place the butt end of a 9-iron on your belt buckle. Next, extend your arms down the shaft. (The clubhead will be down in front of you as it would in your actual address, except the club will be well off the ground.) Now, make the takeaway shoulder turn to just past your right knee. If the club comes off the belt buckle, you've initiated the swing with your hands rather than your shoulders. Done correctly, you'll feel the connection between your shoulder turn and the extension of the forearms. I recommend performing this drill in front of a mirror. When you validate the correct feel with visual feedback, your learning will progress much faster.

your side, and the club shaft should point toward the center of your chest. Begin the takeaway by turning the shoulders and keeping the triangle intact to just past the right foot. The clubhead starts back from the ball on the ball line, then shifts to the toe line as you pivot past the right foot. This clubhead path is known as "straight back." As the clubhead shifts to the toe line, you're developing width away from the ball.

It's possible to take the club *too* straight back. This occurs when a golfer holds the ball line too long with the triangle intact. This action forces the player's arms too far away from the body, disconnecting them from the fluid turn of the shoulders. The result is a swing path outside the Zone.

Done properly, the takeaway follows the ball line and shifts to the toe line. At this point, you're now underway on the upswing.

The middle of the backswing

A crucial movement for keeping the club inside the Zone occurs next: hinging the wrists on the upswing. Here, your hands swing upward as your shoulders continue to turn. The left arm swings across the chest, and the right elbow folds into an "L" position placing the club on an inside path. The club shaft forms a 90-degree angle to the left arm, and the wrists are fully hinged.

The middle of the backswing.

I place a lot of importance on this checkpoint because if you successfully reach this point, staying in the Zone during the rest of the swing is significantly easier.

A common error is to separate your elbows beginning at the mid-point back to the top of the swing resulting in the dreaded "flying elbow" or "chicken wing."

How do you fix this? By maintaining the proper distance between your arms and elbows *throughout the swing*. The distance between your arms at address should remain nearly constant throughout. Here's a great way to test this: Place a Nerf™ soccer ball between your arms at address and take a swing. The ball will ensure that your elbows remain a constant distance apart and help you avoid this common error.

The top of the backswing

All that's necessary to move from the mid-point of the backswing to the top is to continue what you've started. You complete the shoulder turn to approximately 90 degrees from the start. I like the backswing to end with the arms extended above shoulder height. If you look at photos of Tiger Woods' swing, his hands are just above the shoulder. He does not over swing. Instead, he generates great width by controlling the length of his backswing.

The top of the backswing.

The pivot, or turn, ties everything together and is vital to staying in the Zone. The shoulder turn dictates the amount of hip rotation, which is typically half the rotation the shoulders make. A proper turn ensures your weight is properly distributed. At the top of the backswing, most of your weight rests on the inside of your right leg, and your head is behind the ball. (For more discussion of proper weight distribution, read about the reverse pivot on page 59.)

An excellent way to feel the proper shoulder turn on the course is to find an uphill slope and to use a sidehill lie, where the ball is above your feet. Take a few practice swings. The slope dramatizes the feel of a correct inside path made by turning with your shoulders.

HEEL!

The shoulder turn, which is complete at the top of the backswing, raises a footnote for consideration: What do you do with the left heel? At the top of the swing, your weight is primarily on the inside of the back leg. Some instructors teach lifting the heel; others do not. Personally, I'm not an advocate of lifting the left heel for more turn, but if your foot comes up a *small* amount as a result of a *proper* shoulder turn, I won't suggest you keep it down. But here's an important point: Lifting the heel should not be part of your strategy for making a bigger turn. Women tend to do this more than men, believing they get more power from lifting the heel. Instead, what tends to happen is the body rises out of the proper posture resulting in a swing path outside the Playing Zone. Again, if your left heel rises slightly as the result of a proper turn, don't fret. If it rises significantly, my advice is to plant it. It'll be one less moving part you'll have to worry about.

At the top of the backswing, your arms are comfortably extended away from the body with both elbows pointed toward the ground. The width of the swing at this point consists of the extension between your hands and right shoulder, as well as from the shaft and right shoulder. The club is parallel to the target line, not dropping or collapsing these two areas of width. If you lose width here, keeping the downswing in the Zone is difficult.

PRACTICE

Proper width in your swing produces power, yet it's easy to lose width at the top of the backswing if you tuck your right elbow or allow your arms to collapse. Here's a drill to help produce the correct extension and width in your swing. Assume the correct posture at address and extend your left arm as if you're going to grip the club. Place your right arm under the left arm and press the back of the right hand against the back of the left hand. Now, make a pivot driven by the shoulders. This drill provides an excellent sense of how a good shoulder turn feels with the left arm going up and across the chest. This drill also makes a good pre-round stretching exercise.

Tucking the right elbow separates the arms and reduces width and power in your swing.

The downswing

A swing path that remains inside the Playing Zone from the takeaway through the top of the backswing stands a good chance of staying in the Zone through the downswing. Essentially, all that remains is unwinding the turn you've created to this point. That said, timing and tempo are crucial at this juncture. Watch a good golfer and you'll see that she doesn't rush the downswing. Instead, she makes a smooth transition from the upswing through the top and back down again.

The downswing.

Rushing or jerking the start of the downswing contributes to a common error called coming over the top, which is when the clubhead begins the downswing over the right shoulder and the top line of the Playing Zone. This swing path produces shots that fly right or pull left. You can avoid this problem by mastering the proper sequence of events in the downswing.

The downswing begins by allowing your forearms to drop down in a smooth transition. As the arms fall down the path they went up, the clubhead remains behind the hands. Whereas your shoulders initiated the takeaway and brought your hips along in the backswing, your hips initiate the downswing and bring your shoulders along. (Starting the downswing with the shoulders is another cause of coming over the top of the Zone. It may help to think of keeping your back to the target for the first few moments of the downswing.) As you swing, keep your shoulders back but tilt the right shoulder down slightly as your hips rotate left toward the ball. *Do not pull the club.* Simply let it drop as the right elbow swings close to the right hip.

Despite what you may hear, starting the downswing with the hips is not a guaranteed means of bringing the club down on plane.

Done properly, hip rotation helps maintain the shape of your swing, but be careful not to become complacent with this suggestion. Golfers lulled into believing that beginning the downswing with the hips is all they need to know typically over-rotate their hips. Too much hip turn throws the club outside the Zone.

> **QUICK FACT**
>
> What goes up correctly is more likely to come down correctly.

Again, strive to keep the same shape of the swing going down as you used going up—assuming the upswing was on plane—and you'll be in good shape. Will your downswing adhere to the exact same path as your upswing? No, probably not. The natural tendency is to flatten the swing plane slightly as you swing toward the ball, which isn't a problem provided the club stays within the Playing Zone. (If you flatten your downswing too far and the path falls below the Zone, you'll hook the shot.) Some instructors encourage their students to think little of the backswing since the downswing is where your club must be on plane

> **Working on swing fundamentals is the surest way to improve your game.**
> NICK PRICE

to produce playable ball flight. I understand that logic, but it's my experience that keeping a swing on plane, or in the Zone, during the backswing makes keeping the downswing in the Zone much easier.

Impact

Ah, the moment of truth. The impact is the result of all the aforementioned parts coming together in a split second. If you've spent much time around a golf course, you know the sweet sound of

The arms stay together through impact.

the clubface and ball coming together in perfect harmony! At this point, you've uncoiled completely to your starting position. The shaft of the club has swung back down through the toe line then through the ball line. The club is square to the target. As the club contacts the ball, the right arm has fully straightened, releasing its power, and the forearms and shoulders have formed the inverted triangle again. Hopefully, you'll hear that distinctive WHACK of a squared clubface meeting the ball.

A common error is to "break" your arms at impact. When your arms separate during the swing, you diminish the chances of hitting the ball with a squared clubface. Think of impact as the result of all the calculations made until this point. *If your setup is correct, and you swing within the Playing Zone, you're likely to hit the ball square consistently.* Swing over or under the Zone and you're out of position for square impact. The compensations necessary to get the club square are intricate and not easily repeated.

The follow through

From the moment of impact, your body continues to turn as the arms extend down the target line. Your head follows through with your arms, and your back heel rises as your right leg turns toward the target. At the finish, your hips and shoulders face the target. Most of your weight rests on your left hip and leg. Some weight balances on your right foot, which is heel up with the toes pointed at the ground. The arms swing over the top of the left shoulder, as the momentum brings you to a nice high finish.

A nice high finish.

PUTTING IT ALL TOGETHER

A common problem occurs when a golfer tries to think about all the above components—the takeaway, the middle of the backswing, the top of the backswing, the downswing, impact, and the follow through—while swinging.

> A golf swing is more than just a way of advancing the ball. It's a signature.
> PATTY SHEEHAN

The swing takes approximately two seconds, so you have little time to let your mind wander. Focusing your mind prior to and during the swing is the key to tying everything together. How do you do this? With a swing thought.

A **swing thought** is a simple phrase encompassing the many lessons you've learned about swing mechanics. For example, *Make a good turn*, or *Finish to the target* are examples of thoughts that have helped some of my students. Creating your swing thought is best done with the assistance of a good instructor who, after helping you build your swing part by part, can identify the action that ties it all together.

You can also identify your own swing thought at the practice range by sampling several thoughts while driving balls. Ask yourself, *Which thought simplifies the process best and produces the most playable ball flights?* Here are some examples of swing thoughts my students have found helpful:

Smooth takeaway, finish high.

Smooth shoulder turn.

When a player snatches her hands away from the ball in the takeaway—thereby breaking the triangle—a simple drill helps her correct the error. I'll place a two-by-four board behind her club, and this resistance helps her keep the triangle intact—a key start to a correct swing. The swing thought? *Push the board.*

An excellent swing thought to help cure a slice is, *Swing to the hip pocket.* Because slicers swing over the top of the Zone, the thought of swinging to the right hip pocket reminds the player to drop his hands *inside* the Zone rather than over the top. To correct a slice, you want the butt of your club to head for the hip pocket.

In chapter five, "The Pre-shot Routine," you'll read more about the importance of the swing thought and its role in clearing the mind of clutter, thus enabling you to swing smoothly, simply, and accurately.

COMMOM SWING ERRORS

If you follow the instructions above to the letter, your swing would be the envy of everyone with whom you play. But life doesn't work that way. Throughout your golf swing, any number of small errors can occur to produce bad shots. In fact, some errors occur often enough that they have familiar names: the flat swing, the upright swing, or the reverse pivot. The resulting erratic ball flights include the slice or hook, and everything in between, including the occasional straight shot. Since the best way to avoid these problems is to master the fundamentals and to swing within the Playing Zone, I won't go into great detail on each, but I would like to describe what causes the most common errors I see on my lesson tee.

In the **flat swing**, the club travels below the Playing Zone and approaches the ball from the inside. The result is a hook and, possibly, shallow divots to the right of the target. Depending upon the degree to which the path is under the Zone, a golfer with a flat swing may be able to correct the hook by quickly

A flat swing.

squaring the blade before impact, but relying upon this correction reduces the player's margin for error.

GOLF'S ENEMY #1

Take heart if your ball sails left to right without much power: You're not alone. The most common erratic ball flight in golf is **the slice**, and it's caused by an upright swing. But if the downswing above the Playing Zone produces the slice, what causes the over-the-top motion to begin with? Typically, it's an incorrect fundamental, most likely a too-upright posture. If you lack proper spine tilt (45 degrees, bent from the hips), your shoulders are forced to swing level on the downswing. An incorrect grip—perhaps a club held in the palm as opposed to at the base of the fingers—may also cause a slice. *These common errors highlight the importance of correcting your fundamentals before thinking about swing mechanics.*

Sometimes, however, a slice is caused by an uneven swing tempo, especially at the start of the downswing when the slicer tends to rush or jerk the movement.

Left alone, a slicer may try various compensations to correct the weak left-to-right ball flight, including swinging harder, changing the ball position, or aligning well left of the target. Usually these changes make the slice worse.

In an **upright swing**, the club travels over the Playing Zone and approaches the ball from the outside. This swing path produces a slice and sometimes a pull. The outside-in path also produces shanks because of the club's heel striking the ball.

Another common error is the **reverse pivot**, which occurs when a golfer gets out of balance during the swing and reverses the proper weight distribution. Instead of placing most of the weight on the inside of the back leg at the top of the backswing, he places his weight on his front leg and then shifts the weight to the back leg at the finish. The hallmark of a reverse pivot is a wildly inconsistent ball flight

An upright swing.

pattern. The occasional shot may find the target, but a great percentage will fly this way and that. To square the clubface to the target, someone with a reverse pivot must make a number of awkward compensations that create fat shots, thin shots, pulls, pushes, hooks, and slices.

The ball flight is also weak because the momentum of body weight travels in the wrong direction. The irony is a golfer usually develops a reverse pivot by attempting to put more distance in his drive. Somewhere along the way, he heard the misconception that a bigger shoulder turn produces more power, and the double-whammy of attempting a bigger shoulder turn while keeping the head still presents him with a world-class reverse pivot. Remember, you want a better, not bigger, shoulder turn.

Correcting each of these common errors begins with a return

to the basic foundation of the game: the fundamentals. After you've mastered the proper setup, you can then turn to creating a swing path inside the Playing Zone. With proper fundamentals and an on-plane swing, your ball flight will be playable and will sail safely past any of these common errors.

PRACTICE

Practice is vital to improvement in golf and perhaps nowhere more so than in the development of a swing inside the Playing Zone. After you've worked with a mirror or video monitor for visual feedback, take your new swing plane and practice it relentlessly until you develop a feel for swinging inside the Zone.

A key point about practice: ALWAYS aim for a target. Without a target, all learning ceases.

In addition to the million or so practice swings I hope you'll take, here are some drills helpful in improving your swing.

Right-forearm drill. This drill helps develop width and extension in your swing by keeping your right elbow from getting too close to your body. Grip the club with the right hand, and then lay the left hand flat underneath the right elbow. Swing to the top where you'll note your left hand prevents your right elbow from staying too close. This is what proper width and extension feels like.

The broom drill. The broom drill makes use of—surprise!—a broom. It will help you understand the importance of swing plane and of getting the clubface square at impact. Assume the correct posture at address and grip the broom a foot down the handle. Swing back in slow motion. (All swings with a broom should be slow, so no one gets hurt.) As you swing to the top and begin your downswing, the handle will come close to your left side and scrape your ribs if you try to come over the top. By keeping the broom in the Playing Zone, the weight of the broom head will provide the correct feel of a club coming down to the ball from the inside and then extending in front of the body.

Feet-together drill. This drill is great for beginner and high-handicap golfers or for anyone with poor swing posture, a reverse pivot, or a tendency to tilt his body during the swing. It will help you feel the importance of good balance and proper clubhead speed. Place a ball on the tee and take a 7-iron from your bag. At address, place your feet together and swing at the ball with your arms, concentrating on keeping your spine angle correct. Once you separate your feet, you should feel that your lower body is a little quieter.

The full swing is the foundation of the long game. It carries your game off the tee, along the fairway, and, at times, out of bunkers. As you approach the green, your full swing will give way to the varied swings of the short game. Let's turn to that next.

FOUR

THE SHORT GAME

If you want to lower your scores, you can try every new driver or training aid that promises "an immediate and drastic" reduction in handicap; but better scores come from a better short game.

Think about it. A drive, even though it covers a couple hundred yards and more, counts as one shot. Every other shot—all the bunker shots, chips, pitches, and putts necessary to finish the hole—also counts as one shot. On any given hole, your long game comprises one or two shots, and your short game—often called the scoring game—comprises two, three, four, five, six shots…or more.

> The higher the score, the faster you can lower it—with the short game.
> HARVEY PENICK

While some players run up their scores by pin-balling shots around the green, the strong short game player gets up and down.

Even the best struggle with their long games from time

to time. When this happens, *the short game is the glue that keeps a round from falling to pieces.* A professional golfer can have an awful day with their long game but still shoot par, or even better, thanks to the short game. Look at Tiger. When his full-swing shots miss the green, he almost always gets up and down in two shots rather than three. If he hits a full shot that ends up close to the hole, he regularly sinks the putt.

The long and short of my point? For lower scores, *work on the short game!*

In this chapter, you'll learn how to create rock solid bunker shots, chips, pitches, and putts using the proper fundamentals—grip, posture, stance, ball position, alignment, and target awareness. Julie Cole, director of instruction at my school and a former member of the LPGA Tour for 10 years, emphasizes what she calls "a vanilla approach" to the short game.

"The short game gets confusing quickly if you try to keep up with all the fancy specialty shots invented around the green," she says. "Forget flop shots and lobs. Most of us can lower our scores significantly by just understanding how the setup should be compatible with each of the basic short game shots. Nothing fancy is necessary to get up and down." I couldn't agree more.

> The simpler I keep things, the better I play.
> NANCY LOPEZ

A vanilla approach to the short game is simply this: knowing the right shot to use around the green and understanding the correct setup for that shot. This chapter will help you achieve this.

THE SAND

Shots from sand bunkers create unnecessary fear in many golfers. I know how this feels. When I began taking the game seriously, my sand game was awful and I dreaded bunker play. With no control over my sand shots, I'd either leave the ball in the bunker or scull it over the green and into the woods. But once I learned—and practiced—the correct technique, I came to love playing from the sand, especially since it's the only shot in golf where you don't have to worry about hitting the ball. (Instead, you hit the sand, but more on that shortly.)

There are **three levels of sand play**, each with different objectives. Once you are consistently able to meet the goal for level one, start shooting for level two's objective, then move to level three. Here are the objectives.

LEVEL 1: Get the ball out of the trap the first time, every time.

LEVEL 2: Land close to the hole on every shot. Develop
distance control and better touch.

LEVEL 3: Get up and down every time from the sand.

Great sand shots begin with a good setup. For a flat lie, take your normal grip and simply turn the club a little to the right so the clubface points slightly right of the target. This places the club in an open position. Your feet can be a little closer together than normal as you align square to the target. Once your feet are in position, drop your front foot back six inches and then align your shoulders with your feet. This assures you'll avoid the common mistake of aligning *too far left* of the target. Dig your feet in and assume the normal swing posture with your knees slightly flexed, hips and fanny out,

THE CLOCK

Whereas the long game—drives and approach shots—calls for the full swing to cover greater distances, the short game demands more distance control, which is achieved in part by shorter swings.

The degree to which you swing back and through is one way to measure how hard you hit the ball, and "the clock" is a basic tool to explain how high your backswings and follow throughs should be.

To understand how far your hands should travel in the backswing and the finish, visualize standing with your back against a clock face. Your head is on the number 12, and your ball and clubhead are on the number 6. Your shoulders, arms, and club form the upside-down triangle we discussed in the previous chapter.

As you begin the takeaway by turning your shoulders, visualize the triangle created by your arms and shoulders moving along the clock face from 6 up to 7, 8, 9, and ending at 10 for the full swing, then retracing the path back to 6 on the downswing, hitting the ball, and moving up the clock from 6 to 5, 4, 3, and up to 2. That's a simplified way of describing the distance your hands travel for the full swing—from 10 to 2.

In addition to the full swing, the following clock-number combinations—demonstrated in the pictures shown on the opposite page—apply to the short game.

10 to 2: The full swing
Use for drives, approach shots, and long bunker shots.

9 to 3: Pitch shots
Use for 35- to 60-yard shots requiring loft, including short- to medium-distance sand shots. Use a slight shoulder turn and set your wrists to form an "L" with the club and forearms.

8 to 4: Pitch & run
Use for pitch shots to travel approximately 25 to 35 yards. Emphasis is on less loft and more roll than the regular pitch. This swing requires very little wrist set.

7 to 5: Chips
Use for chip shots. Vary club loft and speed to determine the distance covered.

and the back straight and tilted at 45 degrees. Remember: Bend at the hips *not at the waist.*

At address, hold the club two inches behind the ball. Ball position changes depending on the type of shot required: For a high,

In sand shots your club hits the sand, not the ball.

short shot, place the ball just inside the left heel. For a medium-length shot that will roll a few feet after it lands, place the ball in the middle of the stance. For a longer shot that will also roll a few feet after landing, place the ball back in the stance. Some sand shot models advocate taking more sand for short shots and less for long shots. It's difficult to be consistent with this method, and the results can be disastrous. If you need to vary the length and height of the shot, change the ball position first.

If the setup is correct, the natural tendency will be to swing slightly from the outside in, which is the perfect path for a sand shot. Simply swing along the line created by your feet and shoulders. The club should enter the sand about two inches behind the ball. Remember: *In sand shots, you hit the sand not the ball.*

The sand swing is often called a "lazy swing" because you only make a slight shoulder turn, and the tempo is smooth and not too fast. On the clock, swing from 9 to 3 for a short- or medium-distance sand shot. For a long sand shot, you may use the 10-to-2 full swing,

SAND FACTS

Three factors affect the distance of sand shots:
1. Ball position
2. Clubface position (open or square)
3. Length of the swing

albeit at a slower pace. Keep the clubhead accelerating or you'll leave the ball in the bunker. Your hands must always be behind the ball. As you advance past the first level of sand play—getting out of the bunker the first time—start to experiment with the setup by tweaking ball position, the length of the backswing, and the clubface position to see how these small adjustments affect where the ball lands on the green and how it rolls.

Difficult Sand Shots

The previous setup and swing mechanics are for a sand shot from a flat lie. What about the more challenging shots from the sand, such as the buried lie or uphill lie?

Let's start with the *buried lie*, where the head of the ball is barely visible above the sand. With this shot, many golfers make the mistake of swinging the clubhead too close to the ball, which results in a topped shot. In the setup, play the ball back in your stance and close the clubface, perhaps even pointing it a few degrees to the left of the target. Hold the club more upright and hit the sand two to three inches behind the ball and then follow through low by keeping the clubhead below the height of your waist. The ball should pop out low with a good roll. Controlling a shot like this is difficult, and most golfers are happy just to get out of the bunker, which is not difficult using the above technique.

You should also use the buried-lie technique when you find

The "fried egg" lie.

yourself in similar uneven-lie or bad-luck situations, including *"footprints,"* where your ball lands in the footprint of a golfer who forgot to rake the sand, or *"fried eggs,"* where the ball lands in the bunker and scatters a small circle of sand making it look like the yolk in a fried egg. The natural tendency with an uneven lie is to chop or dig, but resist that temptation! The buried-lie setup puts you in the proper position to get the ball out; you don't need to add more angle to your swing.

For the *uphill lie* in a bunker, balance is especially important, particularly if one foot is out of the bunker. An uphill slope increases the loft of your club—uphill shots go higher with less distance—so I suggest using the pitching wedge rather than your sand wedge and also making a longer, fuller swing with a low finish. (Try 10 to 4 on the clock.) Without taking any sand, try a couple of practice swings just to establish your balance and get a feel for the shot.

Perhaps no bunker shot strikes as much fear in an inexperienced sand player as the *downhill lie* in a deep bunker. But with practice and perseverance, hitting the ball on the down slope out of a bunker becomes fun, especially when pulled off in front of friends. Once again, the proper setup is crucial to making this shot. First, align your shoulders with the slope and place your weight primarily on your downhill foot. Position the ball back in your stance with the club square to the target. Begin the swing by getting the club up as steeply as possible in a full backswing (10 on the clock), then swing down the slope and through the sand to a low, partial finish across your body to the 4 position.

PRACTICE

Sand practice should reflect your level of play and help you reach the appropriate objective. For example, if you're just learning bunker play and your goal is to learn to get out the first time every time, you'll find the **Styrofoam cup drill** helpful. A common error for beginner sand players is attempting to hit the ball, rather than the sand. A simple remedy is to cover the ball with a small Styrofoam cup and then work on hitting just behind the lip of the cup. This takes your focus off the ball and forces you to hit a couple inches behind it. When you clip the sand behind the ball (hidden by the cup), it sails right out of the bunker. After 10 shots with the cup, you can return it to its proper use—holding coffee.

Landing close to the hole every time calls for great finesse, and a good drill to improve your sand swing is the **one-handed drill**. Here, you practice swinging with only your right hand. Place your left hand behind your back and then place your ball in an even lie in the sand. Practice 50 shots from this lie to develop tempo and touch in your own "lazy swing."

For the more experienced golfer, the best bunker practice involves hitting hundreds of shots out of the sand from a variety of lies. Want a number? Well, to improve my sand play, I'd hit 250 shots out of the bunker every day, five days a week for several years.

CHIPPING

Your shot has missed the green, but not by much. Your ball is five feet from the edge of the putting surface—it's another 15 feet to the hole from there. In other words, most of the distance in the

For the chip, "grip down" on the club and stand closer to the ball at address. Swing evenly from 7 to 5.

shot is green. When this is the case, it's time to chip.

The chip is an easy shot that can save a number of strokes. With a chip, the ball travels from just off the green with a low trajectory, lands on the green a few feet from the edge, bounces, spins, and rolls the rest of the way to the hole. In the scenario above where your ball has landed five feet from the edge of the green but 20 feet total from the hole, you should aim to hit the ball about eight feet in the air and let it roll the remaining 12 feet, leaving just a short putt—unless, of course, it has gone in the hole. (If you ask a good player about her goal when preparing for a chip, she'll probably say: "My goal is to get the ball in the hole!" I like a bold approach like this.)

Here's the setup for a chip shot: Use the grip you selected from page 25 in "The Fundamentals" chapter—either the overlapping or interlocking grip—but "grip down" on the club. Your right hand should grasp the club just above where the handle meets the shaft. Place the ball in the back of your stance, inside the back foot—this places the hands well ahead of the ball, which is important for solid contact. The feet should be a little closer together than in a normal stance and slightly open to the ball line instead of parallel. Place just a bit more weight on the front foot (60/40 split). A common setup error with the chip shot is to slouch or stand too upright. The posture for the chip should be the same as for the full swing—back straight with a spine tilt of 45 degrees.

It's easy with the chip to lose focus on the target. Select exactly where you want your ball to land, and build your setup around that target. Of course, the eventual target is the hole, but getting there requires landing the ball on a spot so that it rolls to the hole.

Which club should you use? It depends on the distance to the hole. The main factor to consider is, "Which club will get the ball rolling as quickly as possible?" A club with a lot of loft—a wedge, for example—may have too much loft to get the ball rolling quickly. That's fine with a really short chip, where you want the ball to land near the hole and roll a small distance. But for longer chips, you'll want to experiment to find the club that provides the best low trajectory toward the hole.

DEVELOPING TOUCH

While the mechanics must be correct, touch is what's really needed to make your short game great. In other words, think too much about the mechanics of your pitch or chip and you'll likely end up frustrated with the results. Recently I worked with Dennis, a young sales executive with a sound swing, who'd grown frustrated with his chipping.

"I've been playing in number of member-guest tournaments over the summer, and my chips are ruining my scores. I keep double-hitting the ball and taking penalty strokes," he said at the start of the lesson. "I wouldn't want myself as a partner in a tournament."

I set up a chip shot in our school's short-game practice area from 25 feet and asked Dennis to play the ball through. His setup was rock solid, but he'd lost touch in his shot, resulting in an uneven, jerky swing tempo made worse by his use of the wrists for extra push. His fear of double hitting caused Dennis to "tense up," which caused the jerky swing. In an effort to correct the problem, he cluttered his mind with tips on the mechanics of his chip swing, meanwhile losing focus on the target.

"Dennis, put your club down and try tossing the ball onto the green, aiming where you want it to land." I had him complete this drill several times to focus attention on the target and to feel the smooth forward motion necessary for good chipping. Then we picked the club back up and worked on keeping the wrists firm, as well establishing a consistent speed throughout the chip. (Slowing down right before impact then speeding up is what causes double hitting.) Finding a better speed helped Dennis fix the double-hitting problem, but what helped him even more was not over-thinking his mechanics. Target awareness simplified his thoughts, and, today, he's chipping well.

A common error is to get too used to one club for all chip shots. To chip successfully with one club, you have to be deadly accurate. A much better solution is to increase your margin for error

PRACTICE

Good chipping requires touch, experience, practice, and imagination. To develop all four, vary your practice by chipping from a variety of locations around the practice green and from good, average, and awful lies. Can you chip successfully off a tight lie? From a divot? Can you chip successfully to a severely undulating green? The only way to answer "yes" to these is to practice each shot over and over until you get it. When you chip, complete the work by taking your putter out and sinking the putt—that's how the game is played on the course.

The **handkerchief drill** develops your skill at hitting a designated landing area. Begin by spreading several unfolded handkerchiefs in different places on the practice putting green. Then from a good lie, hit 10 chips to each of the landing areas. Hit some shots from an average lie and from an awful lie. The next time you practice this drill, use a different club. An alternative—should you find yourself without a half-dozen handkerchiefs—is to chip to each of the holes on the practice putting green.

The **eyes-closed drill** lets you focus on creating a smooth tempo in your chip. Select a landing area on the practice green and set up to chip to that target. Close your eyes before swinging and concentrate on making a smooth, even chip. Chip 10 balls to each of three landing areas.

by varying your club selection. For practice, try the same chip with a pitching wedge, then an 8-iron, and again with a 6-iron. You'll soon get a feel for which club provides you the right loft, distance control, and roll toward the hole. In my game, an 8-iron works well

> ## The chip is the greatest economist in golf.
> ### BOBBY JONES

for medium to longer chips—say, 20 feet total with eight feet of ground to clear before landing on the green. If the chip is really long, you may try a 5-iron. For short chips, the sand wedge works great because the ball lands softly.

The motion for a chip is a simple, short, pendulum-smooth swing with the shoulders—the triangle of the hands, arms, and shoulders remains intact yet relaxed. Common errors to avoid include tucking or folding the right elbow, "scooping" the ball, or flicking at it with the wrists. If the setup is correct and the stroke is good, contact will be crisp and the club's loft will get the ball airborne. As a rule, the proper degree of swing is 7 to 5 on the clock with the speed of swing and loft of the clubface as factors in how far the ball travels. (That said, really long chips call for an 8-to-4 swing.) Keeping the tempo evenly paced is crucial for chipping.

PITCHING

When faced with more fairway (or rough) than green between your ball and the hole, it's time for a pitch shot. There are two types of pitch shots: the basic pitch and the pitch & run. The amount of carry needed and the amount of green with which you have to work determines the shot you use.

If the hole is cut toward the front of the green allowing very little room for your ball to roll, the **basic pitch** shot is the best option. The basic pitch is a shortened version of the full swing—you swing from 9 to 3 on the clock. The shot travels between 35 and 60 yards. Play the shot with a pitching, sand, or lob wedge. (Club selection depends upon the amount of green with which you have to work. Use a pitching wedge when you have more green and a lob wedge when you have less.) Your objective with the basic pitch is loft and distance. It sounds easy, and is, once you've practiced the proper technique, but the shot actually requires more control than the full swing.

The setup begins by gripping the club as you would for the normal swing. Align square to the target and assume your normal posture and stance. Position the ball in the middle of the stance. (Note: If you need the ball to fly a little higher and stop faster when it gets to the green, open your clubface slightly and place the ball just ahead of center in the stance. For a lower trajectory, square the clubface and move the ball back slightly. Follow this rule for ball position from the middle of your stance: *left for loft, right for roll*.)

Select a spot six feet from the edge of the putting surface. With the correct setup, the pitch

The pitch calls for half of a complete swing with a good pivot and balanced finish.

swing requires rotating the shoulders to where the arms are nearly parallel to the ground, with the wrists set and the club at 90 degrees to the arms. From here, simply make a smooth swing and finish relaxed and balanced. In other words, on the clock you'll swing from 9 to 3, which will set your wrists enough to place the club in the "L" position with your left arm. You may worry that the pitch swing feels slightly outside the plane you've developed for your full swing. This is fine, provided the movement is not exaggerated.

> ## QUICK FACT
>
> If you're ever in doubt as to where to place the ball for a short game shot, position it in the center of your stance.

If the hole is cut toward the back of the green giving you plenty of room to land your shot and roll, the *pitch & run* is the best option. Whereas the basic pitch shot requires much greater distance control, the pitch & run is more forgiving because you have more green with which to work. (In fact, even if the hole is at the front of the green but the ground short of it is firm and the grass is short and uniform, using a pitch & run to land the ball in front of the green is often a safer and less intimidating shot than a higher pitch that must hit its target.) In general, the pitch & run travels between 20 and 35 yards.

The setup is the same as for the basic pitch shot. Pick a pitching, sand, or lob wedge, depending upon the amount of roll you want. (A pitching wedge produces the

> The good chip shot is like the good sand trap; it's your secret weapon.
> TOMMY BOLT

most roll; a lob produces the least.) The swing calls for very little or no wrist set as your hands travel from 8 to 4 on the clock.

Common Pitch Errors

The three most common pitch errors I see in students include "scooping" the ball for extra loft, swinging without a pivot, and letting the club fall behind you. Scooping the ball to get it airborne is a logical thought; however, this action creates a breakdown of the wrists and hands at impact and produces a pitch that's rarely accurate. Scooping is not necessary. Club manufacturers build wedges for all the loft you'll need.

Swinging the arms without a shoulder turn, or pivot, creates a sliding motion and results in shanks and fat shots. You must make a shoulder turn to hit the ball consistently in the center of the club. Finally, letting the club get behind you is an error that results in fat or thin shots. You can avoid this error by swinging along the toe line and using enough wrist set to create the "L" position between your club and left arm (for the basic pitch shot).

PRACTICE

As with chip practice, vary your pitch shots from a variety of distances and from good, average, and awful lies. Also, experiment with ball position in your practice and with different clubs. In addition to the **one-handed, handkerchief**, and **eyes-closed drills**, you may also want to try the **garbage can drill** in your backyard. Place a 55-gallon, plastic garbage can 25 yards away and hit 25 pitches with a sand wedge toward the can, aiming to get the ball in the can. Then move the can to 30 yards and pitch 30 balls with a sand wedge. Continue to vary your distances and repeat this drill with the pitching and lob wedges.

PUTTING

"Putting is the most important part of the game," says Julie Cole, "but you can't convince most people of that." Of course Julie understands the importance of putting. One reason she competed for so long at such a high level is that she sank a lot of putts. Her success was not luck. She spent hours working on becoming an excellent putter, challenging fellow pros to games on the practice putting green and routinely winning.

Putting is golf's great equalizer. A 300-yard drive to the middle of the fairway counts the same as a one-inch putt. (The Scottish shepherds who invented golf either had a bizarre sense of humor or knew that more people would enjoy the game if it was more than just a contest to see who could hit the ball the farthest.)

The encouraging news is that any golfer, of any age, who wants to become a good putter can become one. Putting improvement begins with developing an attitude that draws you from the driving range toward the practice putting green. In more than 20 years of teaching, I've watched a number of students become expert putters, lower their handicaps significantly, and enjoy the game more. These students love to putt. They're not worried about buying the latest drivers because they know the most important club is their putter.

In the previous short game sections, I began with the fundamentals and the techniques. But with putting, I define the characteristics of good putters and poor putters first because the mental approach and frame-of-mind are so critical to achieving success as a putter.

A good putter...

- believes he is a good putter, but still wants to improve.
- strikes the ball consistently in the sweet spot of the blade.
- strokes putts on the intended line, with good speed.
- practices.
- will have had less than 30 putts on a recent round (the average for pros is 29) but feels like he could have putted better.
- finds a comfortable and professionally fitted putter, then sticks with it even when the putts are not falling.
- is consistently excellent.
- understands that even a perfectly struck putt will sometimes fail to drop. (Even the best greens are not marble-smooth.)

Ball should rest below eyes; to check, hold putter under nose and look down shaft.

Best ball position is a putter-head inside the front foot.

When practicing use an alignment device.

The full putting stroke keeps intact the triangle formed between the hands, arms, and shoulders.

The forward swing can be slightly higher than the backswing.

Placing a club under the armpits helps you feel how the shoulders power the putting stroke.

- will not panic over a missed putt—even a short one.
- has a consistent pre-putt routine.
- reads greens consistently well.
- chooses a brand of ball based on how well it putts, not how far it travels from the tee.
- sticks with the chosen line and distance.
- has a smooth and pendulum-like tempo.
- has an air of confidence and contentment. If he misses a putt, he remains confident in his abilities and focuses on the next shot. A good putter lives in the present.
- strokes the ball using the bigger muscles of the shoulders.
- understands that even if his long game is off, putting will keep him in the game.
- spends at least half of his practice time on the practice putting green.
- includes difficult putts in his practice routine.
- wants to be known as a great putter.
- loves to putt.

A poor putter...

- confesses, "I'm a bad putter."
- is terrified of missing putts and addresses the ball with a head full of fears.
- will become angry after a missed putt—so angry it affects him for several shots. (He may even break his putter or helicopter it over the green.)
- rarely practices putting and may never have taken a putting lesson.

- is often only average or worse at other facets of the short game.
- blames missed putts on an ill-fitting putter or poor greens.
- refuses to pay attention to putting fundamentals.
- falls prey to the latest putting tips.
- often has a stroke that is too wristy.
- is streaky.
- thinks good putters are lucky.
- dislikes putting.

If you find yourself more closely described in the "poor putter" list, here's how to make the corrections necessary to become a good putter.

> The better you putt, the bolder you play.
> DON JANUARY

The fundamentals of good putting begin with the grip. Hold your putter in the palms, not with the base of the fingers—exactly the opposite of the full swing. Finding the correct position is easier with the putter since its handle has a flat side. Place the thumb of your left hand down the flat face and place your other fingers so they almost meet the pad of the thumb. (If the grip of the putter is correctly installed, the left hand and the putter blade will now be square to the target.) Place the right hand below the left hand, again with the thumb on the flat part of the grip and the fingers coming around to meet the pad of the thumb. Place your shoulders, arms, and the back of both hands perpendicular to

> A sure way to break a bad putting spell is to get on the practice green and return to the fundamentals.
>
> BOB ROSBURG

the target. Maintain an easy grip pressure—neither too strong nor too loose.

Align yourself square to the ball line. The best putting alignment aid is a carpenter's chalk line, which, with the chalk included, costs no more than $5. If you make a chalk line on the practice green, you'll be forced to understand the importance of standing square to the target and swinging straight back and through.

Put slightly more weight on your front foot for a 60/40 split. Bend your legs slightly and bend over to place your eyes directly over the ball. (Check to see if your eyes are in position by dropping a ball from your nose; it should hit the ball on the green. Or, put the butt end of the putter up to your nose and look down the shaft; you should see the ball.) Position the ball a putter length inside the front foot so that the blade of the putter meets the ball at the bottom of the stroke. This ensures solid contact.

> There is no similarity between golf and putting; they are two different games—one played in the air, the other on the ground.
>
> BEN HOGAN

The shoulders act as the engine for a consistent putting stroke. I teach the *pendulum-style stroke*, driven by the shoulders with the wrists locked because this produces a good roll with consistent speed and direction. Another popular putting style uses the wrists to propel the ball forward, but this method creates inconsistent results. The more motion your wrists make, the broader the possible range of errors. Conversely, the triangle created by the shoulders, hands, and arms in the pendulum-style stroke remains intact throughout the putt, creating better consistency. Furthermore, the lower body remains completely still. Next time you see Tiger Woods putt, watch his lower torso, mid-section, and legs—they don't move. His head also remains still.

If you've been putting mostly with your hands and wrists, try a shoulder-driven putting stroke. It will take a short time to get used to the new feel—and the better contact—but you'll soon discover the path of the putter blade is more consistent and your results will

WRISTY PUTTS ARE RISKY BUSINESS

A "wristy" putt motion is more likely to produce cold streaks. Why? By not keeping your wrists locked, as you do in the pendulum-style putting stroke, you're susceptible to unwanted hand and wrist movement. What happens when you've got a huge putt on the line? You get nervous and your hands shake. The pendulum-style swing eliminates wristiness.

improve. Remember only two variables exist that matter with putting: speed and direction. A good pendulum stroke means consistent speed and consistent direction.

With good fundamentals and a shoulder-driven pendulum stroke, the following can happen:

• The putter's face will be square to the target at impact.

• The speed with which the putter head swings will control the distance of the roll with greater consistency.

A common mistake made in putting is to ignore the importance of target awareness. Of course, the target is the hole, but the best golfers are far more specific than that. They might pick a blade of grass on the left back of the hole or they might think,

> Solid contact is as important with your putter as it is with your five-iron.
> NICK PRICE

"The ball is going to the right edge of the cup." Good putters spend more time looking at the target than the ball, as they dial in the speed and direction of the putt. If you visit a professional tournament, you'll notice that the players treat every putt with enormous respect—even the tap-ins.

Reading Greens

The most common errors I see in putting are rarely due to poor mechanics but instead due to mistakes in reading the green. Unfortunately, most practice putting greens are flat, and, as you know, most course greens are anything but! I like to take beginner golfers to a course green when there's still dew on the grass in the morning. I encourage them to roll balls from a variety of places around the green and at various speeds toward to the hole. Imagine their surprise to watch the lines created by the ball's path. They learn that even on a green with only a moderate slope, few putts are dead straight and that putts can go in from different directions depending on speed.

> The way I putted, I must have been reading the greens in Spanish and putting them in English.
> HOMERO BLANCAS

Learning to read greens takes time and patience, but

if you practice, you'll develop a sixth sense—based on visualization and experience—about the slope on a green. Being able to read a green and find the break point for any given putt is necessary to know how hard to hit the ball. In addition to slope, you'll want to consider the speed of the green (slower greens have longer grass, and the ball tends to roll straighter); the condition of the green (wet weather slows the green down, again causing the ball to roll straighter; a strong wind may affect the ball's path); and the grain of the green (if the grass is leaning away from you, the ball will roll faster and

PUTTING FOR DOLLARS

To the touring professional, a great short game often means thousands of extra dollars a year. Let's look at the final statistics for the PGA's 2001 Tour season. Two well-known professionals, I'll call them Pro A and Pro B, tied for 107th in the greens in regulation rankings—this measures how often a player hits and stays on a green (one shot for a par-3, two for a par-4, and three for a par-5). Both golfers recorded a strike rate of 65.6 percent—for every 18 holes, they hit about 12 greens a round. This means they had to get up and down or a par on six holes each round.

For the same season, pro A ranked 15th in putting; Pro B ranked 131st. Pro A earned $584,072, or 86th in total money earned; Pro B earned $304,644, which placed him 145th on the money list. And by the way, Pro A's average driving distance was 261 yards and Pro B's was 284 yards. A few putts here and a few there and, suddenly, one pro has out-earned the other by almost $300,000. Pro B actually lost his Tour card because only the top 125 money winners each year earn exemptions for all tournaments the following year.

the putt will break less; conversely, putts across the grain tend to break more).

A good putter looks at the entire green and the slopes around it, in addition to the immediate area around the hole. Sometimes, a putt might look like it will break one way when read from behind the hole and another way when read from behind the ball. When a good putter sees different breaks, he goes with the read from behind the ball. If a good putter gets up to the putt and sees something different, he sticks with the initial read.

Some golfers become anxious on exceptionally fast greens. There's no need to panic. Just use a shorter stroke to roll the ball with less pace. If you're able, take a few minutes on the practice green before the round to get a feel for the pace of any given course.

PRACTICE

To become a good putter, sign up for putting lessons with a PGA or LPGA professional and complement the lessons with regular practice. If you're on the practice green, here's how I recommend you spend an hour:

10 minutes: 10-foot putts on a chalk line, swinging straight back and straight through

10 minutes: drills (pages 89-90)

20 minutes: short putts (use the circle drill, page 90)

20 minutes: long putts

In addition, you may choose to purchase a putting matt so you can practice at home, working on the basic stroke, using a chalk line to check squareness of the clubface to the hole during the swing.

Practice drills are especially helpful in putting because repetition builds consistency. The following drills should be part of any putting practice.

One-hand putting drill. Place the right hand on the putter grip and the left hand just off the grip. Stroke five to six putts with a firm wrist from three feet. This drill keeps the body still and the shoulders level and square. Repeat the drill with the opposite hand on the grip.

Blade-behind-the-ball drill. From three feet, place the putter's blade behind the ball, square to the target. Push the ball five times into the hole, using the shoulders and keeping the "triangle" intact. This promotes squareness of contact between the blade and ball.

Club-behind-the-hole drill. This drill develops excellent touch and speed control. Place a club two feet behind the hole, perpendicular to the line. From 15 feet, try to make five putts in a row that end up between the hole and the club; if the ball goes in the hole, count it! Move to 30 feet and repeat the drill. A good variation is to putt to two or even three holes—at different distances on varying slopes.

Short-putt drill. Paul Azinger, one of the best short putters on the PGA Tour, spends hours on the practice putting green. His drill is to make 20 in a row from four feet, then five feet, then six feet. Another drill is to make three from three feet, three from four feet, and three from five feet. If you miss one putt, start over.

Circle Drill. Place five balls in a circle around the hole, each three feet from the cup. Then place another five balls on the same points around the circle at six feet from the hole. Putt the first three-foot putt, then step back to putt the corresponding six-foot ball. Work your way around the circle, first putting the three footer then the six footer before advancing. This drill builds knowledge of how breaks affect the ball's path.

Ladder Drill. The ladder drill involves putting from increasingly longer distances. Start putting from five feet, then 10, 15, 20, 25, and 30 feet. Don't exceed 30 feet. This drill helps you learn to read greens and also shows how the break line in a putt affects the path the ball travels to the hole.

There are several ways to make putting practice more beneficial. First, play friendly games with other putters. The competitive element adds the pressure you'll experience on the course. Second, make your practice difficult. Our practice green has a lot of undulation so students will lean about speed and the various ways putts break. If you're able, find a similar putting green near you.

I teach a putting method based on orthodox fundamentals, a standard-length putter, and a pendulum stroke powered by the shoulders. But if you watch professional golf on TV, you know that the pros, including the most successful ones, use a wide variety of strokes, grips, stances, and putters.

Phil Mickelson stands with his feet open to the line of the putt. Karrie Webb putts cross-handed, with the left hand below the right. Ian Woosnam and countless professionals use the long putter with the butt of the club underneath the chin. Vijay Singh and Paul Azinger use the "belly putter" with the butt end of the shaft in the stomach.

> You don't necessarily have to be a good golfer to be a good putter, but you have to be a good putter to be a good golfer.
> TONY LEMA

Chris DiMarco uses a bizarre-looking grip called "The Claw," where the bottom hand grips the handle with the fingers parallel to the ground. Some golfers hit the ball with a noticeable pop instead of a smooth stroke. Some golfers, like Jack Nicklaus and Arnold Palmer, power their stroke primarily with their wrists and hands instead of the shoulders.

There are a lot of ways to putt successfully. If you've grooved a certain putting style that works through hours of practice, changing it to a more textbook style might not make sense. Putting— more than any other part of the game—will suffer the least by not adhering to a strict set of fundamentals. Ultimately, the putt is about developing touch and while I believe the textbook putting style I teach is the best approach, I certainly recognize it isn't best for everyone.

We've covered a lot of ground in this chapter, so I'd like to review the major points of the short game before moving ahead. Here are the key points for each short game shot.

SAND

- Align square to the target, then drop the front foot back six inches and open the clubface slightly.
- Dig your feet in.
- Place the ball off the inside of the front heel. (Move the ball left of center for loft, right of center for roll.)
- Swing the club on an outside-in swing path.
- Use the full-swing (10 to 2 on the clock) with an even tempo.

CHIPPING

- Grip down on the club.
- Place the feet slightly closer than normal. Open the feet slightly to the ball line and place more weight on the forward foot (60/40 split).
- Stand closer to the ball than for a full swing but maintain good posture.
- Position the ball right of center for roll.

> ## Golf is a game of precision, not strength.
> JACK NICKLAUS

- Keep the hands soft—don't strangle the golf club.
- Use the 7-to-4 swing, keeping the triangle intact back and through with no wrist set.
- Use an 8-to-4 swing for longer chips.

PITCHING

- The two types of pitch shots—the basic pitch and the pitch & run—are determined by the length of the shot (carry) and the degree of roll called for.
- Setup is the same as for the full swing, including aligning square to the target.
- Ball position is in the center. (Left for loft, right for roll.)
- Club shaft swings on foot line.
- The basic pitch involves some wrist set and a swing from 9 to 3.
- The pitch & run keeps the triangle intact with no wrist set on a swing from 8 to 4.

PUTTING

- Set up with your eyes directly over the ball and slightly more weight on your front foot (60/40 split).
- Position the ball inside the front foot.
- Putt using the pendulum stroke, with the shoulders, hands, arms, and putter as one unit. Head and body remain still.

- Keep the clubface square to the target line, back and through.
- Putt on a straight line, never a curved line.
- Learn to read greens to determine distance and direction.

With these points in mind, we can now turn to joining the short and long games together with the cornerstone of consistency, the pre-shot routine.

FIVE

THE PRE-SHOT ROUTINE

A consistent pre-shot routine essentially organizes, condenses, and simplifies everything you know about the putt, chip, pitch, or drive you're about to hit. A solid pre-shot routine also eliminates mental clutter by concentrating your attention on the target rather than thinking about the mechanics of your swing. It ensures your fundamentals will be correct, in turn, increasing the chance of keeping your swing within the Playing Zone and the chance of complying with the ball flight laws. In short, a well-organized pre-shot routine is the foundation of the mental side of golf.

This chapter will help you create and put into practice a consistent pre-shot routine. But first, here's an important point: *Anything you repeat over and over is susceptible to complacency.* It takes work to keep the importance of your pre-shot routine fresh in your mind. If you ever doubt the importance of a pre-shot routine, try this test: Play a round without one!

There are three steps in the pre-shot routine: data, setup, and shot shaping. After the shot, I encourage players to use a post-shot routine, as well, to help them get ready for the next shot. This is especially important after hitting a bad shot.

> You can always find a distraction if you're looking for one.
> TOM KITE

DATA

Whether it's conscious or not, your mind operates like a computer before every swing, gathering various data—sighting the target and determining the distance, for example—and factoring it in to create the shot. Gathering data is the first and most important part of the pre-shot routine, so rather than trust this process to my subconscious, I use the left side of my brain to examine the following:

- Lie of the ball
- Distance to the hole
- Terrain around the ball
  (e.g. uphill, downhill, or sidehill)
- Trouble areas either around the green or on the fairway
- Weather conditions (e.g. wind direction, wind speed, etc.)

This is a lot to take in, yet each part is important because you use the data for a number of critical decisions, including club selec-

QUICK FACT

Obsessive Compulsive? You bet!

Next time you attend a professional golf tournament, follow a player for several holes and pay special attention to his or her pre-shot routine. Notice anything? No, it's not déjà vu. What you're seeing over and over is the same pre-shot routine for every shot.

tion, shot selection, alignment, or swing tempo, just to name a few.

How can you be certain to gather all the data?

Begin by collecting the information well before it's your time to play. While waiting for an individual or a group to tee off ahead of you, start selecting the target line and determining which side of the teeing ground to use. This is especially important if you've never played the course because—like it or not—golf architects work hard to make holes visually distracting.

> Concentration
> is a fine antidote
> to anxiety.
> JACK NICKLAUS

Careful examination of all the data while you wait to play increases the chance of not being tricked by course design.

Golf is a game of great concentration, but it's also a social sport that allows you several hours of uninterrupted time with friends. It takes time to learn how to balance gathering data with talking about last night's bridge game or the shape of the economy. But if you wish to play well, you'll learn to make the most of your pre-shot time. The last thing you want is to stand over the ball with "Please go straight" as the only thought you've had.

SWING AWAY

If you incorporate a practice swing into your pre-shot routine, swing away from the ball. When you step up toward the ball, your attention should be solely on the target.

SETUP

After gathering the data and selecting a club, the setup begins with the approach to the golf ball. *The walk into the golf ball plays an important role in the success of the shot.* Here's how I complete the setup: Start by standing six to 10 feet behind the ball in a direct

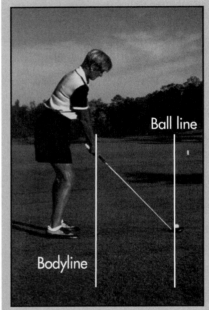

Ball line

Bodyline

Align the shot on the ball line, then approach the ball on the bodyline.

line to the target. Next, select an intermediate target, which is a spot a few inches beyond the ball toward and in line with the target. The intermediate target will help you align the clubface but not your body.

A common error is to focus only on the intermediate target rather than on the real target, which results in aligning the body to the right of the final target. (For proper target alignment procedures, see page 34.)

After selecting an intermediate target, step left of the ball line and walk the six to 10 feet toward the ball on the bodyline—parallel to the ball line—with good posture. Approaching on the bodyline gives you a better view of the final target and makes it easier to line up. As you approach, watch the real target. (Players who focus on the intermediate target while walking toward the ball tend to slouch as they look down, and bad posture is hard to change once you get to the ball.) When you reach the ball, turn and face the ball, *then* look at the intermediate target.

Next, place your feet together and place the club down behind the ball and get into the correct posture. (I always put my feet together because it helps me get into the correct posture, plus determine the correct ball position and stance width.) Establish your stance width with the ball in the appropriate position for the club you're hitting.

At this point, check your fundamentals and look to the target. It's always a good idea to waggle the club to keep from freezing over the ball and to keep your grip

> **Try to think where you want to put the ball, not where you don't want it to go.**
> **BILLY CASPER**

pressure relaxed. (In total, I waggle the club three times before hitting the shot.) At this point, you're ready to enter the third step of the pre-shot routine: shot shaping.

SHOT SHAPING

At this point, the right, or creative, side of the brain enters the pre-shot routine. Here, you envision the ball flying perfectly toward the target.

Shot shaping requires turning off all other thoughts about the setup and focusing solely on the target. If there are hazards between you and the target, ignore them. (Remember: You took note of them when gathering data.) It's at this point that you introduce a swing thought, which is a simple phrase distilling the many lessons you've learned about how to swing properly. An example might be, "Make a good turn and finish to the target." Your swing thought should be mechanically sound and specific to you. When you find one that works, stick with it. I can't emphasize enough the impor-

> **Focus not on the commotion around you, but on the opportunity ahead of you.**
>
> ARNOLD PALMER

tance of using the same swing thought from shot to shot. This helps reinforce the solidity and success of your pre-shot routine.

At this point, if I decide to make any swing adjustments, I step back and restart my routine, paying special attention to the fundamentals. *(Whenever your ball goes off line, always check your fundamentals first.)* Assuming everything is a go, I waggle and then swing the club.

KEEP IT SIMPLE

Note the importance of developing a swing thought, not swing *thoughts*. If you're standing over the ball, thinking, "Correct take-away low and slow with good shoulder turn firm at the top with Tiger-like width then down with the arms just like Karrie Webb and through to the target balanced all the way I wonder where my kids would like to go on vacation this year," then your chances of success are slim.

POST-SHOT ROUTINE

Nearly as important as the pre-shot routine is what happens after you swing, especially if the shot went awry. When you hit a poor shot or three-putt a green, it's easy to lose focus, get tense, or even become angry. A post-shot routine helps you accept the error, analyze what went wrong, and arrive at next shot in the correct frame of mind.

When I make a poor shot, I let myself feel whatever emotion hits me. Usually, I'm upset or frustrated rather than angry. (It's fine to get angry provided you don't act on it by throwing a club or affecting the people around you.) After a couple of seconds, I take a deep breath and exhale, as if to breathe

> If you hit a bad shot, just tell yourself it is good to be alive, relaxing, and walking around a beautiful course. The next shot will be better.
> AL GEIBERGER

the emotion out of me. I accept what went wrong and turn to trying to figure out what corrections to make in setup and swing. I may take a few swings that feel better than the previous shot and then I move on, leaving whatever errors I made behind me.

The key is disciplining my behavior and preventing my emotions from interfering with an opportunity to learn from my mistakes. After all, my mistakes are often my best teachers.

Much of this chapter details my pre-shot routine. You're welcome to use mine, but you'll most likely discover one that's unique to you. Practice your pre-shot routine at the driving range so you can perfect its timing and accuracy. Whatever your pre-shot routine becomes, it should meet the following key points:

- Keep it short. A pre-shot routine should take no more

> Every great player has learned the two C's: how to concentrate and how to maintain composure.
>
> BYRON NELSON

than 30 seconds.

- Make it simple. A pre-shot routine should clear the mind of clutter and let you focus on good course management. Your focus should be on playing the game rather than the mechanics of the swing.

- Make it easily repeatable. The pre-shot routine should be the same every time and should be resilient to pressure.

- Follow your shot with a post-shot routine to help prepare you for the next shot.

SIX

PRACTICE

I get more questions about practice than any other subject. That's a good thing. The first question is usually, "How often should I practice?" My answer: As often as possible! There's a direct correlation between time spent practicing and improvement. The more you practice, the better you get, and unfortunately—as you're probably aware—golf is not like riding a bicycle. If you rarely play and never practice, your fundamentals, timing, tempo, and feel for shots around the green deteriorate.

Most of my students lead full lives, whether they're successful executives, full-time students, or busy parents; and finding time to practice a demanding sport is challenging. But those who schedule practice in their Palm Pilots are the players who are the most consistent.

Another frequent question is, "How much time should I spend playing versus practicing?" Sometimes I think the underlying question is: "Doesn't playing golf also count as practice?" I encourage students to make a distinction between playing and practice. Repetition is important to develop proper technique, and no one in your foursome will be overly forgiving the third time you line up the exact same putt. Plus, it's difficult to focus exclusively on improvement while playing.

> **Practice puts brains in your muscles.**
> SAM SNEAD

The best golfers establish a balance between time at the practice facility and time on the golf course. They've also learned how to make the most of their practice time so that the hard work creates success on the golf course. When I work with aspiring professionals, amateurs, or juniors, I have to remind them that balance is also important when it comes to activities besides golf. If I failed to set aside time for non-golf activities, I'd be in my office or on the practice tee all day, seven days a week. My schedule includes time to play golf, time to practice, time for physical fitness, but also time for relaxation, spiritual renewal, and fun with friends.

In earlier chapters, I shared drills and practice recommendations to help you improve specific aspects of your game. In this chapter, I put the big picture together and prescribe realistic practice schedules for three types of players: the *weekend player* who wants to improve his game, the *aspiring amateur*, and the *aspiring Tour player*.

Each program should last a minimum of 12 weeks. Research indicates that most people stop a new exercise program by the sixth week; however, it takes 12 weeks of exercise before significant success can be measured. The same is true with golf. Even if you're practicing several hours a week outside of playing, signs of consistent improvement take time to appear. In addition to making a 12-week commitment, write down specific goals and track your progress in a journal. Referring to your journal will provide encouragement along the way.

> **Preparation through steady practice is the only honest avenue to achieving your potential.**
> CHI CHI RODRIGUEZ

THE WEEKEND PLAYER PROGRAM

If you play primarily on the weekends but would like to see your level of play improve, you'll need to spend at least two hours a week practicing. But before you rush off to the driving range, I suggest committing to a series of lessons with an instructor—see chapter eight, "Choosing a Good Teacher," if you're looking for one—to help you identify areas to work on, set realistic goals, and maximize your practice time.

You may choose to start your 12-week program with one or two one-hour lessons, where you should ask your instructor to identify three areas in your swing—the takeaway, impact, and follow through, for example—that need work. After two weeks of practice, return for another hour lesson to chart your progress and identify additional improvement areas. Throughout a 12-week program, I suggest the following lesson schedule to my students:

- *Four one-hour lessons*
  (one before the program, then spaced every two weeks)
- *One short-game clinic*
- *Two one-hour, follow-up lessons*
  (spaced two to three weeks apart)

For individual practice, set aside two days a week at a minimum as "practice days," when you'll visit the course or range with the express purpose of practicing. Playing with friends does not count, because you're less likely to focus on improvement when enjoying the camaraderie. Plus, if your friends know you're practicing, they'll be apt to provide advice.

Ideally, you should spend two hours per practice session. Since this is unrealistic for most of us, the following recommendation is based on two one-hour sessions a week with one session spent exclusively on the full swing and the second on the short game. Here's how to spend the hour on the *full swing*:

10 minutes: Stretch your back, shoulders, arms, and legs. (See "Stretching" on page 117.)

45 minutes: Work on the full swing, giving equal balance to hitting with woods and irons. Practice the swing three to four times in between hitting the ball. Use a mirror to check your posture and fundamentals, and work with alignment aids as you vary your targets. Pay special attention to your tendencies. Constant improvement is the goal during this practice time, so you can "take it to the course." Measure your progress with a journal.

5 minutes: Stretch and take a few moments to assess what went well during practice and which parts of your game need work.

Each night: Spend 10 to 15 minutes working on indoor drills prescribed by your teacher.

For the *short game practice* session, I recommend the same format, with the middle 45 minutes spent on two skills, one of which must always be putting. In other words, spend 22 minutes working on chipping and 23 minutes on putting one week, then 22 minutes on pitching and 23 minutes on putting the next week. Always check with your instructor for specific drills. For my suggestions, refer to the recommended drills in chapter four, "The Short Game."

> Most golfers prepare for disaster. A good golfer prepares for success.
> BOB TOSKI

A common error beginners make is trying to practice too many elements of the game in one session. Your mind cannot focus on 10 items at once, so it's best to focus your energy on just one or two skills per practice session. Place an emphasis on quality not quantity.

THE ASPIRING AMATEUR PROGRAM

Many of the golfers I work with are good players, fortunate enough to be able to play often—in many cases, golf is how they build customer relationships in business. They post solid scores consistently and perform well in their annual club tournaments. When a player of this caliber wishes to improve his game, perhaps to the level of winning state-level amateur tournaments, I prescribe a 12-week program that touches every aspect of his game.

> Never practice without a thought in mind.
> NANCY LOPEZ

Within this group, there are two types of players, each with different lesson schedule needs. The first player needs little work on his swing. His fundamentals are sound, and he's diligent about practice. For this player, I suggest the following lesson schedule to take his game to the next level:

- An hour lesson prior to the program to define goals
- An hour lesson six weeks into the program to check the swing
- An hour lesson at the end of the 12-week program to evaluate the success

The second player aspiring to become an amateur is one whose swing needs to be rebuilt to take her to the next level. This player has probably developed some compensatory moves in her swing to make up for weaknesses in her fundamentals. Often, this player's grip needs to be changed, and she'll need more instruction during the course of her 12-week improvement program. I recommend the following lesson plan for this player:

> Correct one fault at a time. Concentrate on the one fault you want to overcome.
> SAM SNEAD

- An hour lesson prior to the program to review fundamentals and goals
- An hour lesson every two weeks through the completion of the program

The aspiring amateur's weekly practice schedule is the same, regardless of the lesson plan. Note that I've inserted suggested drills, but ultimately, you should work with your instructor to define drills applicable to your game.

MONDAY

4:30–5:30 p.m.   Putting practice: Circle drill, from three and six feet (see page 90), Ladder drill (see page 90) Long putts(30+ feet): uphill and downhill

5:30–6:30 p.m.   Full swing: Right-forearm drill (see page 60) The broom drill (see page 61) Feet-together drill (see page 61) Full swing (hitting the ball)

TUESDAY

4:30–5:15 p.m.   Irons and woods: 10 balls each club, varying targets

5:15–6:00 p.m.   Greenside bunker shots: 10 short, 10 mid, 10 long, 10 from difficult lies

WEDNESDAY

4:30–6:00 p.m.   Wedge work: Handkerchief drill (see page 75) for distance control. Pace off yards 10, 20, 30, and 40.

THURSDAY   *Game day* Play nine holes: Goal is par or personal best

FRIDAY

4:30–6:00 p.m.   Putt and chip: Up and downs: Choose five different pins from difficult lies. Hit five balls to each pin and putt them in. Handkerchief drill: (see page 75) for distance control

SATURDAY &

SUNDAY: *Game days*

HOW DRILLS DEVELOP TOUCH

The drills I describe in earlier chapters and refer to in these practice regimens are crucial to your improvement as a golfer. Drills develop touch, which is the sixth sense that all good golfers possess, especially in and around the greens. A player with a great sense of touch knows how to select precisely the right club for a chip or knows how to hit a pitch shot 15 yards instead of 18 or 12, all without thinking.

I offer one caveat: Drills for the full swing help you become proficient with the elements that go into the full swing, but there's a tendency for students to become drill proficient and swing deficient. It's important to focus on the big picture as well. Ultimately, I want students to play golf, not perform drills.

THE ASPIRING TOUR PLAYER PROGRAM

What about the player who wants to make a living playing golf? The following intensive plan requires a great deal of time and effort, but it includes time for balance. Even if you are aspiring to be a great professional golfer, life cannot be all golf all the time. I have included time for exercise, spiritual reflection, or simply going to the movies. If you plan to play at this level, you'll need a full-time coach overseeing every aspect of your game.

MONDAY

6–7 a.m.	Meditation/prayer/positive reading material. Visualize success in your game.
7–8 a.m.	Workout: stretching, cardio, and strength training
8–9 a.m.	*Breakfast*
9–12 p.m.	Full swing: repetition practice with focus on your swing tendencies
	Irons and woods: 250 to 300 balls, target focus
	Video/drills and use of applicable teaching aids
12–1 p.m.	*Lunch*
1–4 p.m.	Play 18 holes alone with two balls. After your drive, place one ball in the woods or similar troublesome spot and play both through.
	Keep stats and note your trouble shots for discussion with your teacher.
4–5 p.m.	Putting: 100 three-foot putts left to right, downhill
5–10 p.m.	*Dinner* and evening activities
10:00 p.m.	Lights out

TUESDAY

6–7 a.m.	Meditation/prayer/positive reading material
7–8 a.m.	Workout: stretching, cardio, and strength training
8–9 a.m.	*Breakfast*
9–11 a.m.	Short sand shots from different lengths and lies landing within six feet of target

TUESDAY, CONTINUED

11–12 p.m.	Putting: 100 six-foot putts; 25 each from four different angles
12–1 p.m.	*Lunch*
1–4 p.m.	Play 18 holes of situational golf alone with two balls.
4–5 p.m.	Putting: 30-foot putts uphill and downhill
5–10 p.m.	*Dinner* and evening activities
10:00 p.m.	Lights out

WEDNESDAY

6–7 a.m.	Meditation/prayer/positive reading material
7–8 a.m.	Workout: stretching, cardio, and strength training
8–9 a.m.	*Breakfast*
9–12 p.m.	Full swing drills as assigned by instructor, including hitting five balls with each club to alternate targets, plus 100 55- to 60-yard pitches landing within six feet of your target
12–1 p.m.	*Lunch*
1–3 p.m.	Chipping: five balls up and down 20 times from 20 yards; again, from 30 yards
3–5 p.m.	Putting drills as assigned by instructor
5–10 p.m.	*Dinner* and evening activities
10:00 p.m.	Lights out

THURSDAY

6–7 a.m.	Meditation/prayer/positive reading material
7–8 a.m.	Workout: stretching, cardio, and strength training

THURSDAY, CONTINUED

8–9 a.m.	*Breakfast*
9–12 p.m.	Play 18 holes of situational golf alone with two balls.
12–1 p.m.	*Lunch*
1–4 p.m.	Play a round of 18 holes alone.
4–5 p.m.	Putting: 100 three-foot putts; 25 four-foot putts from different angles
5–10 p.m.	*Dinner* and evening activities
10:00 p.m.	Lights out

FRIDAY

6–7 a.m.	Meditation/prayer/positive reading material
7–8 a.m.	Workout: stretching, cardio, and strength training
8–9 a.m.	*Breakfast*
9–12 p.m.	Greenside bunker play from bad lies. Play five balls up and down from sidehill, downhill, uphill, hard pan, and high-rough lies.
12–1 p.m.	*Lunch*
1–4 p.m.	Full swing: 200 to 500 balls, alternating targets. Focus on your swing enhancements.
4–5 p.m.	Putting drills as assigned by instructor

SATURDAY

Play 18 holes with friends. Rest, relax, and have fun.

SUNDAY

Rest.

I imagine that the weekly practice schedules of Tiger Woods, Annika Sorenstam, David Duval, Karrie Webb, Justin Leonard, and all the great professional golfers look pretty similar to the one above. This type of regimen is what it takes to play difficult courses and routinely shoot 67.

In summary, practice is the only way your game will improve. If you go out and shoot a low score after not playing or practicing in many months, your success is most likely due to having an uncluttered mind. Your expectations are low and you're relaxed. But try to repeat that performance over and over, and you'll likely realize your game has not miraculously improved while you were away.

Remember these four key points about practice:

1. Set specific practice objectives.
2. Focus your attention on one or two skills to improve.
3. Vary your practice with different clubs to different targets and from different lies.
4. Use drills to develop touch.

There is nothing in this game of golf that can't be improved upon—if you practice.
PATTY BERG

SEVEN

PHYSICAL FITNESS

Golf is not an aerobic activity—the sport won't pump your heart or work your lungs the way basketball and soccer will. But golf is a physical activity. If you forgo the golf cart, you're walking four to five miles, and walking is one of the greatest forms of exercise. Carry your bag, and those miles become an even better workout. Even if you use a cart, a full round may take four hours or more to play, and each time you swing, you're using muscles in the shoulders, back, arms, hands, stomach, hips, and legs. Those who simply write off golf as a leisure activity are forgetting that, first and foremost, golf is a *sport*. And the better shape you're in, the better you'll play this great sport.

You do not have to be an Olympian or a tri-athlete to play well; in fact, you can be a great golfer without fitting any of the preconceived notions of what athletes are *supposed* to look like. That's one of the many reasons I love golf—it's accessible to people of all shapes and sizes. But, regardless of your build, athletic inclination, or physical condition, you'll find following a complete fitness program—one that includes stretching, cardiovascular, and strength-building exercises—will

> If there is a fountain of youth, it has to be exercise.
> GARY PLAYER

improve your game and more importantly, your overall quality of life.

Specific to your game, you can expect the following benefits from a fitness program:

- better rotation in your swing
- better distance
- better posture in your setup
- better accuracy with fewer swing compensations
- a reduced risk of painful or recurring injuries
- more energy on the back nine and during long practice sessions

In this chapter, I share some stretching and strength-training exercises, plus general healthful living suggestions that I've picked up during my career. They've improved my life both on and off the course. I am not a medical doctor, licensed physical therapist, nutritionist, or qualified personal trainer, and my writing is not intended as a substitute for advice or treatment that you may have received from any

> No matter how talented a player is, they will never reach their true potential unless they are willing to take the necessary time to stay physically fit.
> BUTCH HARMON

such professionals. *Before starting this or any other physical fitness program, consult with your doctor about the appropriateness of the program for you.*

With that in mind, let's look at the various ways to build a healthy, flexible, and strong body to give you an extra edge on the golf course.

DO AS THE PROS DO

There's little evidence to suggest that the great golfers of long ago exercised, but beginning in the 1950s and 1960s with Ben Hogan, Sam Snead, and Gary Player, rigorous practice and exercise grew in popularity. Today, it's the touring professional who isn't working out who is the exception. In fact, most pros on tour manage to squeeze in four to five aerobic sessions each week, even while playing in tournaments.

S-T-R-E-T-C-H-I-N-G & THE WARM UP

A common complaint I hear on the golf course is, "My back is stiff and sore." That's hardly surprising since the swing is a twisting motion that puts great stress on the upper and especially lower back. If you're quite young—less than age 30 or so—you rarely feel the effects of this torque on your back. But as you age, no matter how gracefully you do it, your muscles lose range of motion, and a tight back is going to let you know when it's been pushed or pulled beyond its level of comfort. Moreover, tight muscles shorten your backswing, resulting in shorter drives. Lengthening (and strengthening) your muscles, especially those in the shoulders, back, and arms, provides you with better range of motion that generates more clubhead speed.

QUICK FACT

A healthy muscle can stretch more than 1.5 times its length.

Stretching before every workout session—as well as before you practice or play—keeps your muscles loose and limber while lessening your chance of injury. I warm up before stretching to increase the blood flow to the muscles. Five minutes or more of moderate aerobic activity—jogging in place, jumping jacks, walking, or anything that builds a light sweat—typically works. I also stretch after working out to help my muscles process the lactic acid built up by exercise.

Here are some general rules about stretching.

- Stretch slowly without bouncing. (Bouncing can result in hurting a muscle.)
- Perform two or three repetitions for each stretch, holding each for 15 to 20 seconds.
- Do not stretch through pain. (If something hurts, I report it to my doctor.)
- Breathe deeply through stretching. Do not hold your breath.

Before I work out and after warming up, I perform, at a minimum, the following basic stretches.

LOWER BACK: Begin with the "pelvic tilt" by lying on your back with knees bent, feet on the floor. Tighten your buttocks and stomach muscles, then push your lower back flat against the floor for five seconds. Relax and repeat five times. Then, hold a pelvic tilt while bringing both knees to your chest with your hands. Slowly pull your knees toward your shoulders and hold for five seconds. Rest and repeat.

LOWER TRUNK: Lie on your back with your knees bent and together, feet on the floor, and arms out to brace yourself. Slowly roll your knees to the left, as far toward the floor as you can, keeping your shoulders on the floor. Hold for 15 seconds, then repeat on the opposite side.

UPPER BACK: Get on your hands and knees—hands under shoulders, knees under hips—and look at the floor as you tuck your chin in and arch your back, pushing your stomach down to the floor. Hold for 15 seconds, then relax. Next, round your back up, like a cat stretching after a nap, and drop your head toward the floor. Hold for 15 seconds, then relax. Next leave your palms on

Stretching the upper back.

the floor and roll back onto your feet, then push your arms out as far as you can in front of you.

SHOULDERS: Roll your shoulders forward and backward with your arms at your side, then repeat with your arms extended parallel to the ground.

SIDES & HIPS: Place your left hand on your hip and reach to the sky with your right arm. Slowly bend your torso to the left, reaching for the horizon. Switch hands and repeat on the opposite side.

HIPS: Lying on your back, cross your legs as if sitting in a chair, then grasp the "under" leg with both hands and pull the knee toward your chest until you feel the stretch in your buttocks and hips. Repeat on the opposite side.

CALVES & HAMSTRINGS: Lie flat on your back through a

Stretching the hips.

doorway with the doorframe against your left hip. Keep your right leg flat against the floor and raise your left leg until your left heel rests against the doorframe. Your left leg should form a right angle to your right leg. Hold the stretch in your hamstring. To stretch your calves and Achilles tendon, use a towel, belt, or dog leash to pull your toes toward you. You can also keep your right leg flat against the floor and pull your left leg (kept straight) over to the floor on your right to stretch your IT band and hip muscles. Repeat for the opposite leg.

Another option is to sit with your left leg extended forward, your right foot flush against the inside of your left thigh and pull your left foot back toward you until you feel a good stretch in the calf. (If you can't reach your foot with your hands, use a towel to pull the foot backward.) To stretch the hamstring in the same leg, lean forward and grasp your left instep, pulling yourself down into a stretch. Repeat for the opposite leg.

GAME-DAY STRETCHING

A full stretching regime is not always realistic before a round. Here are the "bare-essential" stretches, which take only a few minutes.

- **Warm up** by walking quickly from your car to the clubhouse and to the course.
- **Hamstrings and lower back:** Place your feet just a few inches apart and gently reach for your toes with your knees slightly bent.
- **Back, sides, and hips:** Take an iron as in the picture below and hold the club above your head. Slowly bend your torso to the left and stretch, then to the right.
- **Back and trunk:** Stand with your feet slightly more than shoulder-width apart, place a club behind your shoulders and extend your arms off both ends. Turn slowly as far as you can in both directions and hold the stretch.
- **Shoulders:** Slowly roll your shoulders forward and back.

QUADRICEPS: Stand and hold onto a chair or wall and grasp your right ankle, pulling it toward your buttocks. Repeat on the opposite side.

STRENGTH TRAINING

I've heard it all when it comes to strength training and golf. *Don't lift weights—it'll ruin your swing.* Or: *You don't need muscle to drive the ball.* And: *Bulk up and you'll lose flexibility, range of motion, and feel.* These are misconceptions.

Strength training, complemented by stretching, will improve your swing and help you drive the ball farther by improving your posture, range of motion, flexibility, and feel for the ball. The training I prefer is not intended to *build* muscles. Instead, it's meant to develop the muscles, tendons, and ligaments used in the swing. Rather than losing the feel for your swing, strengthening muscles specific to golf gives you better balance, coordination, and *control* of your swing. Before I began a weight training program, I could never feel my back and shoulder muscles. When I make a shoulder turn today, I can feel those muscles. That awareness helps me control them.

Another misconception I hear is, *I'm too old to lift weights.* In fact, older people benefit most from a carefully monitored strength training program because it helps build bone density.

> I run about five miles a week, and lift four days a week using a light and heavy combination of weights.
>
> DAVID DUVAL

With these benefits in mind, here's how I use strength training to increase blood flow, work through a functional range of motion specific to golf, and strengthen the tendons and ligaments in every joint of my body. Remember: I am not a personal trainer. You should consult a doctor first and then a personal trainer to create a program specific to your needs. The general rules I follow include:

- Perform each movement slowly and smoothly.
- Use moderate weight, favoring more repetitions (12 to 15) each set versus higher weight and fewer reps. Perform two or more sets of each exercise.

• Inhale during the easier portion of the exercise and exhale evenly during the difficult part.

• Allow at least a day of rest between strengthening the same muscle groups. Your muscles need to recuperate.

My personal routine involves the use of a product called the Total Gym™, which is a machine that stores easily in my home and allows me to strengthen nearly every major muscle group. (There are similar products on the market, but if you're interested in learning more about the Total Gym, you can call 1–800–541–4900, or visit *www.totalgym.com*.) When I worked out in a gym, I used a combination of free weights and machines, but in general, I preferred machines because they limit range of motion, thereby reducing the risk of injury. Assuming you'll work out in a gym, here are the exercises you can use and the muscles they work.

LOWER BODY: QUADRICEPS, HAMSTRINGS, HIPS, BUTTOCKS, AND CALVES: Start with the **leg press**, which mimics a freestanding squat exercise. This works the hamstrings, quadriceps, buttocks, and muscles in

The leg press.

the hip. The leg press can also be used to work your calves by moving the seat away from the foot platform, placing your toes on its edge, extending your legs, and moving the weight forward and back with the calf muscles.

The *leg extension* machine works the quadriceps (the front muscles of your thigh) and involves extending your legs in front of you with resistance from the machine against your shins. The *leg curl* machine works the hamstrings. You lie on your stomach and "curl" your legs up by pushing against the pad with the back of your ankles.

MID-SECTION: ABDOMINALS AND LOWER BACK: Ah, the dreaded mid-section…an endless source of frustration for many of us, especially as we age. The best way to strengthen the stomach muscles is by performing variations on the tried-and-true sit-up. The *abdominal crunch* involves lying on your back, hands touching gently behind your ears, knees bent, and feet on the floor. Slowly lift your chin to the ceiling and tighten your stomach,

The abdominal crunch.

pushing it down into the floor. I also like **side crunches** where I roll on my side, bending my lower arm to hold my "love handle" area, as in the picture on the following page. I "crunch" the side stomach muscles by raising my torso toward the sky. To strengthen the lower back, I use the *pelvic tilt*, described in the stretching exercises.

Upper Body: Back, chest, shoulder, and arm muscles: For the upper back, try the *seated row* machine. With your chest against the

The side crunch.

pad, pull the weight toward you, keeping your elbows back. The machine works the major muscles of the upper back, as well as your shoulders and upper arms. Other machines good for the upper back include the *seated pull over* and *torso/arm* machines. You can work chest and upper arm muscles with the *chest press*, but many trainers tell me there's no better exercise than *push-ups*. Work your shoulders with either a machine—*the lateral raise*—or with free weights held by your side as you perform *shoulder shrugs* forward and backward.

For biceps, the *arm curl* machine works the major muscles in the front of my upper

The seated pull over.

125

MY PERSONAL ROUTINE

Making time for workouts when you're busy is challenging, but I've found a program that takes just 30 minutes a day. It's based on Bill Phillips' best-selling book, *Body for Life* (HarperCollins Publishers, $26). (This is a great book, but I feel it lacks full coverage of several essential topics, including stretching.) Essentially, I alternate between cardiovascular and strength training three days a week. On Mondays, Wednesdays, and Fridays, I complete 30 minutes of strength training, alternating between the upper body muscles one day—Monday, for example—then the lower body on Wednesday. Friday, it's upper body, then lower body the next Monday.

On Tuesdays, Thursdays, and Saturdays, my cardiovascular training on the treadmill or elliptical trainer consists of 10 minutes warming up, then 20 minutes of increasing speed every two minutes up to 10 minutes. Then I start over again, building intensity every two minutes up to 20 minutes. For example, I start jogging at five mph, then increase a half mph every two minutes until I reach seven mph at 10 minutes. Then I restart at five mph and increase again every two minutes until the 20 minutes are up. Then, well...I'm exhausted.

arms. Then move to the *triceps extension* machine to work the back of your upper arms. For wrists and hands, try a *coil spring handgrip*.

These are just a few of the many ways you can strengthen the muscles used in golf. Entire books have been written on the subject of fitness and golf. Two I recommend are *The GOLF Magazine Golf Fitness Handbook* by Gary Wiren and *Total Conditioning for Golfers* by Neil Chasan.

CARDIOVASCULAR CONDITIONING

As you work out, your heart and lungs deliver oxygenated blood to your muscles. The better shape you're in, the better your body delivers oxygen-loaded blood as the exercise lasts longer and builds in intensity. Even at rest, a conditioned body is more efficient at delivering nutrient-rich blood to the muscles than is a body that's not fit.

> All hard work brings a profit, but mere talk leads to poverty.
> PROVERBS 14:23

Fortunately, getting in shape isn't *that* difficult. You need only commit to exercising at least three times a week for no less than half an hour. You can walk (briskly), jog, hike, bike, in-line skate, ski, swim, attend an aerobics class—anything that gets your heart rate up and keeps it up for the duration of the exercise. Ideally, your heart rate should run between 60 to 90 percent of your maximum heart rate, which is determined by subtracting your age from 220. (If you're 50, your max is 170, and you should try to keep your heart rate between 102 and 153 beats a

A STORY I'LL RUN BY YOU

After tearing ligaments in both knees, undergoing orthopedic surgeries, and doing nothing more vigorous than walking fast for 15 years, I decided to set an ambitious goal: to run a 10K. I consulted my doctor and bought a book on running, from which I learned the correct fundamentals, including the right stride for someone of my height and body shape. I started slowly—adding short jogs to my walking routine—but eventually progressed to running more. I bought a treadmill to reduce the stress on my knees and body and trained using the correct posture, breathing, and techniques for running up and down hills. Then, on a cold and rainy day in January—six months after starting my training program—and on a hilly course, I finished the race in 61 minutes.

When I was training for my run, I thought about and worked on the fundamentals from the running book. But when it was time to

run the race, I wasn't thinking about stride, breathing, posture, and other running technicalities. I trusted my training and simply ran. The same reliance on training applies on the golf course, where thinking too much will ruin your game. You have to trust your practice.

minute. To determine your heart rate, take your pulse for six seconds, then multiply that figure by 10.)

I use a combination of fast walking and running because I like to be outdoors, but I have plenty of friends who prefer to get their cardiovascular training at the gym on the treadmill, Stairmaster, or stationary bike. It doesn't matter where or how you do it, just *that* you do it.

NUTRITION/DIET

My experience is that few golfers think about how what they eat affects their performance on the course. Even in popular sport magazines, nutrition and better golf are rarely linked. That surprises me since food is fuel for your mind and body and if you want to stay strong over the last few holes of the back nine, you'd better pay attention to your diet.

FLUID IN, FLUID OUT

When you sweat, you lose water, which must be replaced. How much should you drink? On non-workout days, take your weight, divide it in half, and drink that number in fluid ounces. (A 100-pound person would drink 50 fluid ounces.) Ample water is essential to good health. Water lubricates your joints and flushes lactic acid, reducing stiffness and soreness.

When you work out, you need to drink even more. Drink fluids before, during, and after physical activity. Water suffices for most activities, but for particularly long workouts—those lasting an hour or more—you might try a sports drink like Gatorade®, which contains carbohydrates and electrolytes for energy and endurance.

Here are some general rules I follow in my own diet:

- Eat at least three meals a day and never skip breakfast.
- Eat more meals (every three to four hours) with smaller portions.
- Eat larger meals earlier in the day and progress to smaller meals at night.
- Eat a well-balanced diet with at least one food from each of the four major food groups—dairy, meat or fish, fruits and vegetables, and grains (breads and cereals).
- Drink as much water as possible, at least 48 ounces a day.
- Make room for the occasional treat!

Like golf, nutrition is subject to a flurry of recommendations. But a good diet needn't be complicated. If you eat a relatively balanced diet, you'll have all the carbohydrates, protein, iron, calcium, and sugar you need to have energy for a healthy and fit lifestyle.

REST & RENEWAL

The rest I get every evening and on days when I limit physical activity is just as important to my mental and physical health as exercise. Every night, I strive for at least eight hours of sleep to allow my body to reset from the day's events and stresses. Physical exercise helps me go to bed sleepy. I'm careful, however, not to lift weights or work out strenuously two days in a row. Your body needs time to recover from strenuous exercise.

The most important part of my life—the part that contributes most to my overall well being—is my deep Christian faith. I've noticed that the most happy and successful people I've met also have some deep faith that helps put life's experiences into perspective. What is a bad day on the golf course or at work if your life is enriched by something much more important?

WORK THE KINKS OUT

I'm an advocate of neuro-muscular therapy, or massage, and I visit my massage therapist every couple of months. I prefer deep tissue massage, but even a light massage can be helpful to your golf game. Benefits of massage are many and include increased blood flow to the muscles. This allows them to receive oxygen and nutrients and expel lactic acid and other waste products more efficiently. Massage also reduces heart rate, lowers blood pressure, increases blood circulation, relaxes muscles, improves range of motion, and even releases endorphins. Be sure to find a qualified massage therapist, preferably one that's certified by a well-recognized group like the American Massage Therapy Association.

TYING IT ALL TOGETHER

Despite the perception that golf is a game of leisure, my hope is you'll see that it's a sport that demands the best performance you can give and that your ability to play well is increased by improving your level of fitness. Think of it this way: Your body is the most important piece of equipment you own, and spending $500 on a new driver makes little sense if your range of motion is limited. Investing a few hours a week in stretching, strength training, and cardiovascular workouts will improve your game more than a new Titanium driver.

If you start and stick to a program that includes these elements, plus incorporates general healthful living tips, you'll soon find your drives go farther, thanks to a better backswing and increased clubhead speed at impact; your accuracy improves because of better posture and increased muscular control; your swing is less likely to make you sore or cause injury; your endurance on the back nine is improved due to increased energy; and your scores drop with increased confidence.

> Fitness plays an important part in mental discipline—being tired coming down the last holes can lead to letting a few shots slip away.
>
> DAVID LEADBETTER

The most important thing I wish for any of my students is not an improved swing, a dazzling short game, or a lower handicap. It's that they find happiness. If you incorporate changes in the areas described in this chapter—again remembering to get suggestions from your doctor or personal trainer—you'll feel younger and more limber, and you'll soon find yourself greeting life with more vigor and joy.

EIGHT

CHOOSING A GOOD TEACHER

As a professional golf instructor, I believe in the importance of taking lessons from a golf pro, whatever your level of play. My students are often surprised that I take lessons. Instruction keeps my fundamentals in order and helps me spot minor problems before they become major. If Tiger Woods takes lessons—and he takes plenty—then every golfer should take lessons!

I wish I could promise that my book is all you'll ever need to play golf successfully. It's not. *(Be skeptical of any book or product that promotes itself as the only thing your game needs.)* This book helps

> Don't be too proud to take lessons. I'm not.
> JACK NICKLAUS

you develop a rock solid foundation through attention to the fundamentals. An instructor will help build upon this foundation, and this chapter will help you find an instructor.

How often should you take lessons? In a perfect world, we would all be like players on the Tour, always practicing under the watchful eye of a coach and instructor. But that takes money and, more precious, time. Instead, strive to find an instructor who will help you define your improvement goals and then match those to a realistic instruction schedule that takes into account your budget and time demands.

QUICK FACT

Seventy percent of children who took organized lessons stuck with the game into adulthood; only 30 percent of kids who "picked up" the game played into adulthood.

Source: National Golf Foundation

A new golfer, of any age, who takes her first baby steps in the gentle nursery of a golf school under the care of a professional, is much more likely to stick with the game. The well-taught beginner often develops a lifelong affair with the game. The numbers prove this. A recent National Golf Foundation study detailed that 70 percent of children who took organized lessons stuck with the game into adulthood, whereas only 30 percent of children who simply "picked up" the game played into adulthood. I also intuitively believe that children who take lessons early and stay with the game also continue to receive instruction into adulthood.

In most sports, participants begin playing on teams where they are taught by coaches. The instruction usually continues through high school and even college. One important reason the average handicap has not changed in the past 20 years—despite amazing advances in equipment technology—is that too few people take instruction.

If I've convinced you to head for a lesson, here's what you need to know to find a good teacher.

MY FIRST LESSON

When I was 17 and became interested in golf, my father took me to Joe Cheves, the head professional at Mimosa Hills Golf Club in Morganton, NC, where I grew up. My father, who's a good golfer to this day, never took lessons as a beginner, and he realized that, with lessons, he could have become better earlier. So it was with his encouragement that I went to Joe, a well-known, disciplined instructor and outstanding golfer. Joe taught me the fundamentals and insisted that I practice them until they were second nature. Without his direction, I may have become discouraged and quit. Instead, in just five years, I went from my first lesson to trying to qualify for the LPGA tour. My natural athleticism helped, but my career would never have happened without those hours spent on Joe Cheves' lesson tee.

First, not all teachers are equal. Golf instructors who are particularly dedicated to their careers will pursue membership in the Professional Golfers' Association of America (PGA) or the Teaching & Club Professional Division of the Ladies Professional Golf Association (LPGA).

These professional organizations foster excellence and ongoing education. Members have passed a difficult playing test (that admits only one out of every four applicants) and have completed a long apprenticeship. While there are good teachers who have chosen to bypass membership in the PGA or LPGA, you can be assured of consistently good instruction from a teacher with PGA or LPGA affiliation.

What else should you look for in a teacher? It's my belief you should have a teacher who:

- stresses the fundamentals
- keeps things simple
- asks about your goals or helps you set some before any instruction begins
- defines the tangible ways your progress will be measured
- is busy with at least 10 hours of lessons a week. (Teachers with a full book usually have a sharp eye and well-honed communication skills.)
- focuses solely on you and your needs during the lesson
- has the ability to understand quickly how you best learn— whether by feel, sight, or hearing
- makes you feel at ease on the lesson tee
- emphasizes the need for patience and practice in learning
- likes people and has a passion for the game
- takes lessons herself

TEACHING THE TEACHER

Teachers who take lessons themselves are in a unique position to understand their student's needs. I love taking lessons. It's good for my game and good for my career as a teacher. When I've scheduled a lesson, I drive to the range, warm up, and stretch. Interestingly, I'm always a little nervous because I want to perform well, so I understand when someone arrives at my lesson tee with butterflies. If you're able to find a teacher who also takes lessons, you'll appreciate how much better they understand your needs as a student.

Where are the good teachers? You'll find them in numerous places, from small public courses to sprawling resorts with several golf courses. Begin your search by asking fellow golfers if they know of anyone who's shown dramatic improvement. That person probably worked with a successful teacher. You can also simply ask if people know of a good teacher in your area.

In addition to contacting the PGA—(561)624-8400 or *www.pga.com*—or the LPGA—(386)274-6200 or *www.lpga.com*—for member instructors near you, you can visit the library to check out the annual "top instructor" lists from GOLF *Magazine*, *Golf Digest*, or *Golf for Women*. Each of these magazines ranks the nation's top 50 or 100 instructors and breaks them out by regions, and their lists are consistently reliable.

Don't despair if you learn that a great teacher works out of a private club. Many private clubs allow non-members to take lessons from their professionals. You may also want to investigate a local golf school since schools tend to offer group beginner lessons led by two or three teachers, giving you the opportunity to select the instructor you like best for future lessons. One advantage of finding a teacher at a golf school is they're likely to be teaching often—one of the characteristics of a good teacher.

Look for a teacher who likes people and has passion for the game.

> Tutorage under a competent instructor is worth more than the slight remuneration you will pay him.
>
> SAM SNEAD

YOUR FIRST LESSON

Your first lesson with an instructor is also part of your search for the right teacher. If you don't like him or her, you don't have to return for another lesson! Since all learning ceases without a target, I hope you'll sit down with your instructor either before the lesson begins or in the first few moments to identify your golf goals. An accomplished teacher will help you define those goals, and just as importantly, help you determine how to measure your progress toward meeting them.

At the beginning of every first lesson with a new student, I thoroughly evaluate the following:

- *Mental golf baggage.* What's in the student's head that will compete with the instruction to come? I know people who've been playing for 20 years who still believe things they heard when they first started—misconceptions such as keeping the left arm stiff or the head down.

- *Equipment.* If a student has poorly fitting or outdated equipment, they won't improve. The teacher helps the student find properly fitted clubs and encourages the student to stick with them.

- *Physical attributes and/or limitations.* Are there any back ailments? Is the student particularly flexible or inflexible, tall or short, large or thin?

• *Fundamentals.* Does the student use the correct grip, posture, stance, ball position, target awareness & alignment?

HOW TO BE A GOOD STUDENT

The success of a lesson isn't entirely up to the teacher. You need to be a good student, as well. Approach each lesson open minded and willing to change, if necessary. When Bob Toski told me that I'd better change my grip if I wanted to play professionally, I sure felt like moving on—especially after my booming drives became weak shots to the right—but I stayed on his tee. I wasn't taking lessons to hear how good I was. I was there to hear what I needed to improve and to get better. I had to be open to change.

Willingness to change is the first step toward being a good student.

Being a good student also means accepting that improvement in golf takes time. You cannot expect to take a lesson, practice a few times, then step to the tee and play well for the rest of your days. In fact—if you change something as fundamental as your grip—you can safely assume you'll step to the tee and play worse for a while, until you've practiced and played enough to "get it." Patience is essential to taking lessons. Make the most of your investment in

> Always keep learning. It keeps you young.
> PATTY BERG

lessons by asking for drills from your teacher and then practice, practice, practice.

It's important to make a commitment to your instructor's learning model. Joe Cheves, my first teacher, gave me the following advice in my first lesson: "In golf, there are more teachers than players." He was right about all the teachers. I received endless advice from well-intentioned, high and low handicappers, especially leading up to my trial at Q-School.

Is Your Instructor Helping?

I wish there were a sure-fire way, without taking a few lessons, to identify if an instructor is a good fit for you. But it takes time to get to know each other and build trust, and that cannot happen by any method other than going through a few lessons together.

That said, there are ways to gauge, early on, if your instructor is going to be helpful. Here are several criteria:

- Your teacher should work with you in the first or second lesson to identify your goals.
- Your teacher should be approachable and enjoy your feedback.
- A good teacher takes a personal interest in your game.
- Your teacher should take time before and after the lesson to highlight the key points you're working on and how they fit into your overall improvement plan.
- You should see and feel some improvement by the end of the first lesson. If you're undergoing a change in your grip or in another fundamental and your game is getting worse, the instructor should talk you through the process by explaining why things are getting worse on the road to improvement.

- If you're practicing and following the teacher's advice, and improvement is not happening by the third lesson, talk with your instructor to clarify the objectives and ensure that you understand the techniques she's teaching.
- If you still have not improved by the fourth lesson, try finding another instructor.

People learn differently, just as teachers teach differently, and not every teacher will work well for every student. That said, most instructors I know are well suited to their jobs. They are patient, good communicators, and they know and love the game.

Do not get discouraged if you start with a teacher who does not work out. With little effort, you'll find another instructor who will help you improve.

It takes time for a student and teacher to develop a partnership, but when it happens, improvement follows quickly. If you're just starting with a new teacher, especially if you're a beginner, you'll want to take more lessons in a shorter period of time to build trust. If you're interested in improving but are no longer a beginner,

> What you might learn in six months of practice, your pro can tell you in five minutes.
>
> JACK BURKE, SR.

you may find a lesson every six to eight weeks is sufficient to prevent your fundamentals from deteriorating. If you're an advanced golfer with a low handicap, perhaps you'll benefit from only three or four lessons a year.

One of the greatest benefits I enjoy from teaching is getting to know my students over a long period of time. I've been blessed by many friendships that arose from my role as a golf instructor. In my opinion, a good golf teacher cares about more than the student's golf game and will express interest in how life is going off the course. (Of course, many of my students prefer to focus strictly on golf, and that's a boundary I'm happy to respect.)

I'm honored that so many fine people ask me to help them achieve their golf goals. In exchange for their trust, I share everything I know about how to play better golf. My students tell me that if they take my teaching to heart, they improve. Ultimately, teaching is empowerment, and a good teacher empowers students with the confidence to go to the course and enjoy the game. If you've found someone who empowers your game, stick with him or her. You're right where you need to be.

NINE

FINDING THE RIGHT EQUIPMENT

The correct fundamentals provide a greater chance of keeping your swing in the Playing Zone (the swing plane that produces playable ball flight). I've addressed this in great detail, but there's another crucial element—your equipment. To make the most of an excellent setup and a good swing, you need to play with a set of professionally fitted clubs. Your putter, wedges, irons, fairway woods, and driver should all be purchased after talking with a PGA or LPGA professional or an accredited clubfitter, since properly fitted clubs allow you to maximize your natural ability and personal swing characteristics.

If you've heard that only professionals or low-handicap golfers need custom-fit clubs, perhaps you'll be surprised to learn that less-experienced golfers need custom-fit clubs even more than better players. An experienced golfer is able to adjust to a poorly fit club, whereas an inexperienced golfer is less attuned to the compensations necessary to hit the ball square. Regardless of your level of play, properly fit clubs improve your shots.

Moreover, if you play with poorly fitted clubs, you'll find it difficult to assume the correct position at address and you'll have to make awkward adjustments in your swing to get the clubface square at impact.

Here's some good news: It's not always necessary to purchase the most expensive clubs in order to complement

OLD GOLF CLUBS NEVER DIE...

They just get handed to someone else. If you're a beginner and you've received a set of second-hand clubs, it's fine to take them to the course to see if you'll be interested in learning this great sport. After you decide to take your improvement seriously, I suggest writing a thank-you note to whomever gave you the clubs, then put them in the attic.

QUICK FACT

The right equipment is the equipment that's custom-built for your body shape, swing, and natural ability.

a solid swing. A $200 driver with the correct shaft flex and loft will often be more effective than a $500 driver purchased directly off the rack. The same applies to wedges, irons, fairway woods, and putters. If your teacher believes some of the clubs in your bag will keep you from becoming consistent, and thus maximize your enjoyment of the game, then it's time to buy new clubs. The best clubs for your game should be purchased as soon as you get serious about golf. The right clubs will last for years.

If you fill a room with professional clubfitters, the conversation will sound like rocket science to most of us. That said, here are a few key words and concepts you'll want to understand:

SHAFT FLEX: Shaft flex is the degree to which your club shaft bends. A flexible shaft, obviously, bends more than a super-stiff shaft (also called a Tour-stiff shaft). It's important that your shaft flex match how fast you swing. Typically, a stronger player needs a stiffer shaft. John Daly, one of the longest drivers on the PGA Tour, uses an extremely stiff shaft in his clubs. A slight female beginner will probably need the most flexible shafts available. Most male golfers should use regular flex shafts.

LOFT: Loft is the angle between the clubface and the ground. A driver has the least loft—usually around 10 degrees—and the lob wedge has the highest, up to 64 degrees. The higher the loft, the higher the ball will travel in the air with the shortest distance. The lower the loft, the farther it will travel on a lower trajectory.

LIE: The lie is the angle at the hosel (where the clubhead joins the shaft), which forms the angle between the shaft and the clubhead. A lie that's too upright creates pulled shots that may hook. A too-flat lie produces pushed shots that may fade. In general, taller players need more upright lie angles, and shorter players need flatter lie angles.

CLUBHEAD SPEED: The clubhead speed is the velocity of the club at impact. For most men, it's between 80 and 90 mph. For Tour-playing men, it's 110 mph or more. For women, it averages 75 mph. The higher your clubhead speed, the stiffer the shaft you need. Someone with low clubhead speed needs a very flexible shaft.

When the grip size, length of the shaft, shaft flex, and lie angle are correct, the club is properly fitted.

WHERE TO HAVE YOUR CLUBS FITTED

When I opened my school in 1987, few equipment companies offered custom-fitted clubs, but today, almost all the club manufacturers can tailor their clubs. It's always been easy for me to find clubs because my height (six feet) enables me to generate a lot of clubhead speed, meaning men's clubs have worked well for me. But what about the five-foot-tall female amateur who can't generate the speed necessary to swing a man's club effectively? What about the male golfer with short arms and a long torso? What about the eight-year-old girl excited about the game but currently lacking strength?

TO PICK UP THE RIGHT CLUBS, PUT DOWN THE EGO

On a recent trip to Myrtle Beach, I was playing golf with my friend and teaching associate Julie Cole, and the starter paired us with two young men. At the beginning of the round, one of our new companions made a point of telling me he was playing with clubs fitted with *Tour-stiff* shafts, as if his level of play demanded clubs fitted for the less-than-five-percent of male golfers who generate clubhead speeds of around 110 mph. Perhaps he believed his Tour-stiff shafts would make him play like a pro. Unfortunately, his shafts had the opposite effect, and he sprayed the ball all over the course. The moral of this story? You'll be a lot happier in your game if you purchase equipment fitted specifically for your swing rather than believing you should have what the pros use. When your clubfitter asks how far you hit the ball off the tee, give him an accurate number. Then, he'll help you actually reach the "fudged" distance.

Or the recently retired executive with the replaced hip who's determined to realize his lifelong dream of five rounds weekly the rest of his life?

Fortunately, none of these people has to worry about finding the right equipment. Many PGA and LPGA teaching professionals can custom-fit clubs, and just as many have excellent relationships with name-brand manufacturers. All well-trained instructors can tell if a club isn't properly fit. Your teacher knows your swing, and this knowledge is essential in fitting clubs. If your teaching professional isn't a trained clubfitter, he or she will know someone who is and can call to discuss your swing with the fitter. Many golf stores—from huge emporiums to much smaller retail outfits—offer custom fitting and, perhaps more importantly, have a knowledgeable custom fitter on staff.

If you can't find a teaching professional or a professional clubfitter, ask several good golfers in your area for a referral. The trade associations for clubfitters are the Professional Clubmakers Society and the Golf Clubmakers Association. Members attend association meetings and stay abreast of the latest developments and technologies.

When I recommend custom fitting, I'm talking about all the clubs in your bag—not just the irons or the driver. If a clubfitter is helping you with new irons, for example, ask him to take a look at the rest of your clubs. Your woods, wedges, irons, and drivers should fit your swing. As the most important club in the bag, your putter should be just the right length if you're going to have a successful scoring game. That putter will be in your bag for years, so make sure it's neither too long nor too short.

THE CLUB FITTING PROCESS

If you're the type to put off dentist appointments because they're unpleasant, you'll be relieved to know a professional clubfitting session is painless. What can you expect? Here are the basic components of a clubfitting:

Clubhead speed check. The clubfitter will clock your swing speed and gauge your swing tempo (slow, medium, or fast) to determine the amount of shaft flex you need. The faster you swing, the stiffer the shaft. He'll also use your swing speed to pick what material—steel or graphite—from which to make your shafts. According to Stan Roach, the professional clubfitter with my school, if your swing is between 50 and 82 mph, graphite shafts work best. Swing speeds from 83 to 87 mph call for shafts of either graphite or steel, and players with swings faster than 88 mph should use steel shafts.

Club length. To determine the ideal club lengths for you, a clubfitter will check several variables. First, he'll begin with a static measurement, such as the distance from your fingertips to the floor, your wrists to the floor, or your knuckles to the floor. The next variable is your posture, both at address and throughout the swing. He'll use the posture analysis and static measurements to arrive at an initial suggested club length. Then, using pressure-sensitive tape on the clubhead, he'll measure how consistently you hit the center of the clubface at this length. Finally, he'll vary the clubhead weight for any additional compensation.

Dynamic lie angle. Your ideal lie angle, or the angle between the clubhead and the shaft, comes from working with four factors, namely shaft length, clubhead speed, shaft flex, and the lie degree (or loft) of the clubface.

Grip size. A grip too small or too large for your hands may cause you to clamp down on the club, causing your wrists to freeze up and your upper and lower arms to tighten. This prevents the club from setting properly at the top of the swing and also from releasing properly at the finish. In simple terms, this tension causes poor ball contact and bad shots. The clubfitter will measure your hands and examine your grip to find the correct size.

Driver Measurements. When it comes to the driver, every player has his or her optimum loft, shaft length, and flex. To determine the driver's ideal loft, a clubfitter needs to know your ideal launch angle at impact. (The launch angle, which is the angle at which the ball leaves the clubface in the first few feet, will lie between 10 and 14 degrees.) Whereas golfers with clubhead speeds of more than 105 mph need less loft from a lower angle for more distance, the proper rule for most golfers is that more loft equals more distance. Driver length is determined with pressure-sensitive tape. The distance at which the golfer consistently hits the "sweet spot" is the length the clubfitter selects.

> Acquiring a new set of golf clubs is rather like getting married. The honeymoon is wonderful, but how things go after that depend on whether the courtship has tested the true compatibility of the partners.
> PETER DOBEREINER

When you purchase new equipment, know that it takes a few rounds to "break in" or get used to new clubs. It's unrealistic to expect instant improvement with them. But if they have been properly fitted, they'll soon produce excellent results, provided your fundamentals are correct and you have a sound swing or putting stroke.

TEN

THE FRAMEWORK FOR CHANGE

My father introduced me to golf. He loves the game and wanted me to love it, too. To make sure I learned properly, Dad insisted I begin with lessons. He loved the phrase, *Plan the work and work the plan*, and by sending me to Joe Cheves, my first instructor, he was ensuring that I'd have a plan to follow. Throughout my career—especially when I was a junior player—Dad would ask, "Are you working your plan?" Usually, that meant, *Have you practiced?* But sometimes, he was gently reminding me that focus and commitment to one model of improvement were the routes to success.

> Pop didn't just teach me golf. He taught me discipline.
>
> ARNOLD PALMER

During the past 20 years, I've spent more than 20,000 hours (give or take a dozen) helping people develop plans for improvement. One of my students, a business executive, referred to me as a "turnaround specialist," because the parallels between his job—examining what a company is doing incorrectly, creating a plan for correction, and overseeing the implementation of that plan—and mine were similar. Whenever he returned for a lesson and admitted he had failed to practice, I'd say, "Now, David, what happens to a company when it stops working its plan?"

"It goes under," he'd admit with a sheepish grin.

Fortunately, your golf game will not "go under" if you fail to develop and work a plan for improvement. Improvement may be slow or nonexistent, but you won't lose your job as a golfer.

That brings up an important point. I know plenty of weekend golfers who cannot remember their last lesson, yet they enjoy the game more than golfers so maniacally focused on their plan that they forget to enjoy the process. Golf is the greatest game, and it's a privilege to play it. When I get frustrated, remembering that golf is fun helps put that frustration in perspective.

You've bought this book or checked it out from the library. You're obviously interested in improving your game. *Rock Solid Golf* provides you with a plan for improvement. Now begins the action part. Reading a book is an intellectual exercise. Making the transition to action takes three things:

- *commitment*
- *discipline*
- *patience*

As you lay down this book and think about making the changes necessary to improve your game, you'll need to make a **commitment** to the process. Some of my students find it helpful to write their commitment in their practice journal. One man I taught wrote, "I commit to my plan for improving my golf game for the next 12 weeks," on a yellow stickie. He wrote the date on it and placed it on his bathroom mirror.

"Every time I took a shower, it would fall off the mirror, so I taped it up with clear packing tape," he said. "It'll be up there long after my 12 weeks end. Maybe I won't stop at 12 weeks!"

He kept going, and when I last saw him, he gushed about leading the field by several strokes in his club's annual member-guest tournament.

"Two years ago, I came in dead last," he reminded me.

Once you make the commitment, **discipline** is the glue that keeps the process together. Sometimes on the lesson tee, I wish for a magic wand to fix a student's swing so she could suddenly hit a drive 250 yards straight down the fairway or hit a 5-iron perfectly. But there are no shortcuts to getting better.

> You can't improve unless you change what you are currently doing.
> GARY WIREN

If you've spent your life lacking discipline—constantly making pledges to improve, starting out, then giving up when the work became dull—does it mean you're doomed to give up on this, too? No!

I've worked with many students who have confessed to dropping diets after a week or making good on their New Year's resolutions only until January 2, and yet they've stuck to their plans and are much better golfers as a result. Once invigorated by the success of improving your game, you'll realize discipline is not so difficult after all. Perhaps, you'll apply that discipline to other areas of your life.

> **To improve is to change; to be perfect is to change often.**
>
> WINSTON CHURCHILL

But—and there's always a "but," isn't there?—the key to everything in this book is **patience.** Lasting change takes time. I measure improvement in golf over years, not weeks or months. Accepting this allows you to relax and enjoy the process. Wherever you are in your game right now is exactly where you are, and who knows what tomorrow may bring?

When working your Rock Solid plan for improvement, what tomorrow brings may feel like regression rather than improvement—especially if you go through a fundamental change such as your grip. With changes to your fundamentals, I can almost guarantee you'll get worse before you get better. I call this *lesson progression.*

Lesson progression is less discouraging for my high-handicap students than it is for my advanced players. Many experienced golfers who visit my school feel they've hit a wall and need a fresh approach to reach their full potential. If I find a weakness in their fundamentals, I insist on fixing it. When these players make the change to follow a more orthodox model, they shoot higher scores at first and typically lose confidence in their game. This is normal. For proof, let's look at the best golfer in the world.

After winning the 1997 Masters, Tiger Woods told his coach, Butch Harmon, he was pleased with his game but knew he needed a better swing to win more tournaments and more majors. He wanted to realize his full potential. In the months following the 1997 Masters, Tiger and Butch worked day after day building a new swing. Meanwhile, Tiger continued to play tournament golf, and while his play wasn't poor, it wasn't brilliant. Eighteen months after initiating the plan for improvement, Tiger's swing became second nature, and his staggering results have amazed fans, the media, and his fellow professionals on Tour.

> I can sum it up like this. Thank God for the game of golf.
>
> ARNOLD PALMER

Many other fine professional golfers—Nick Faldo and Mark O'Meara, just to name two—and thousands of regular players have completely rebuilt their swings and found success. The pattern is always the same: A golfer reaches a certain level, restructures his fundamentals, goes backward, and then exceeds his former abilities.

Sometimes, when I change a student's grip, the club feels like a hammer to him, and the ball goes everywhere. Sometimes that will be the last time I'll see him, and, if so, I typically consider that my fault for not successfully communicating lesson progression.

Expect lesson progression as part of your plan, and it will be less threatening.

If you take one thing from this book, I hope it's this: *Nothing is as important for a lifetime of success in golf than developing and maintaining the proper fundamentals.*

'Maintaining' is the critical word here. Every great golfer, including Tiger Woods, constantly monitors the fundamentals. If your fundamentals are consistently excellent, you will play consistently well. Getting your swing inside the Playing Zone, developing a rock solid short game and pre-shot routine—all these are important, but none is possible without a foundation built upon the proper fundamentals.

My hope is you'll use the Rock Solid plan to improve your game, but, more importantly, I hope you come to enjoy the game more than ever. The book is complete. It's now your turn to write. I would love to hear about your progress.

Write to:
Dana Rader
Dana Rader Golf School
Ballantyne Resort
10000 Ballantyne Commons Parkway
Charlotte, NC 28277
Or to: danarader@aol.com

Thanks and God bless.

APPENDIX

PRACTICE JOURNALS

Keeping a practice journal is one the best ways to measure improvement and identify areas that need attention. There are no right or
wrong ways to journal your progress, but I do suggest you write it
down. Without a photographic memory, you'll find the detail too
difficult to track in your head. Further, taking time to write after
practicing forces you to reflect and ask, *what went well today? What
caused me the most trouble?*

Throughout the book, I've discussed the importance of practicing with a specific objective. *Without a target, all learning ceases.*
Practicing with one objective is more realistic than trying to work
on several objectives at once. How do you determine what needs
your attention the most? One way is to work with your instructor
to identify opportunities for improvement. Another way is to use a
playing journal.

The Playing Journal

How you play determines what you practice. **After each
round of golf, take the time to enter the following statistics into
your journal.** (You'll be able to use this book as a start but eventually, you'll need a notebook for additional space. Many of my students use their personal computers to design their practice journal.)

Playing Stats	Date	Date	Date	Date	Date
Greens in regulation					
Penalty strokes					
Fairways hit					
# of putts for each hole					
Up and downs					
Sand saves					
Ball striking*					
Course management**					
Putting***					

*Ball striking is a measure of how well you're hitting the ball. Enter either "on line" or "in trouble" to track how solidly your clubface is contacting the ball.

**Course management is not just comprised of your pre-shot routine but also includes how well you play the short game, your use of imagery in shot shaping, club selection, and your overall strategy in playing the course. It's a subjective observation. Enter "Good," "Fair," or "Poor," as an analysis of how you felt you played the course.

***Putting is also a subjective observation arising from the number of missed putts that should have been holed and the number of putts on a given round (recorded above as an average). Enter "Good," "Fair," or "Poor." Bear in mind that how you feel you putted is not always accurate. Nonetheless, record your feelings to look for ties between attitude and performance.

Weekly Practice Journal

Using the observations from your playing journal or direction from your instructor, identify one or two areas of your game to practice per session. Write your objectives down and record the drills you performed toward meeting that goal. Then, record your progress, including your personal evaluation of how well the session went.

Date	Goal	Drills Performed	Progress/Observations

Julie Cole's Pin Ball Game

Julie Cole, whose short game was the foundation of her success on the LPGA Tour, developed the following practice game to improve the art of getting up and down.

Use a putting or pitching green and select a position off the green with a shot to all the holes. Use a variety of clubs and try to get the ball up and down from the same place to each hole consecutively. Record the number of attempts for each hole before going to the next hole. For example: if you make a two on a hole, record your score and progress to the next hole. However, on any hole that you do not get up and down in two, keep score until you putt out, then start over on that hole (continuing to add to your score) until the hole is completed with an up and down in two.

	Score
Hole #1	_____
Hole #2	_____
Hole #3	_____
Hole #4	_____
Hole #5	_____
Total	_____

Score this game once a week. (Note that professional status is scoring 2 or fewer shots for each hole.) In the above example with five holes on the practice green, a perfect score equals ten or less. Use the following grid to record your success over a year.

Pin Ball Score Card

Month	Week 1	Week 2	Week 3	Week 4
January				
February				
March				
April				
May				
June				
July				
August				
September				
October				
November				
December				

GLOSSARY OF TERMS

(All of these definitions assume a right-handed player.)

ADDRESS: the position you assume prior to swinging the club. Technically, it occurs when you've taken your stance and placed your club on the ground. At address, all of your fundamentals—grip, posture, stance, ball position, target awareness & alignment—should be correct.

AMATEUR: typically a very good player who plays for enjoyment rather than money. Can also mean a complete novice.

APPROACH SHOT: any shot from off the green toward the hole.

BACKSWING: the backswing is the portion of the swing beginning with the movement of the club away from the ball to the top of the swing.

BACK NINE: the final nine holes of an 18-hole round.

BALL FLIGHT LAWS: a set of five physical laws that govern ball flight. Developed by Dr. Gary Wiren, a noted golf researcher and instructor, the laws determine how the path, speed, and angle of approach of the clubhead, plus the centeredness and squareness of the clubface, determine the flight of the ball.

BALL LINE: an imaginary line intersecting the ball and target. A proper pre-shot routine involves aligning shots along the ball line, then approaching the ball along the bodyline.

BIRDIE: one stroke under par on a hole.

BODYLINE: an imaginary line formed at the toes at address and running parallel to the ball line. A proper pre-shot routine involves aligning shots along the ball line, then approaching the ball along the bodyline. Also called the toe line.

BOGEY: one stroke over par on a hole.

BREAK: the degree of curve a putt makes as it rolls on a putting green.

BUNKER: sand hazard. Also known as a sand trap. A greenside bunker is one directly beside the green.

BURIED LIE: the lie of a ball where some portion of the ball is below the surface. See also fried egg and footprint.

BUTT: the large end of the shaft where the grip is installed.

CARRY: the distance the ball travels in the air.

CHIP: a short, low-flying shot to the green.

CLOSED FACE: the clubface faces left at address, strikes the ball to the left at impact, or faces skyward at the top of the backswing. Generally results in a shot that lands to the left of its intended mark. Also known as shut face.

CLUBFACE: the flat end of a club

CLUB LENGTH: the measure from the butt of the grip to the bottom of the clubhead.

CLUBHEAD SPEED: the velocity of the club at impact.

DIVOT: the hole created when the club makes contact with the ground.

DOGLEG: a left or right bend in the fairway, typically placed where the average drive would land.

DOWNHILL LIE: when your right foot is higher than your left when addressing the ball.

DOWNSWING: the portion of the swing when the clubhead is moving toward the ball.

DRIVE: played from the teeing ground, it's the first shot on a hole.

DRIVING RANGE: an area set aside for hitting practice balls.

EAGLE: two strokes under par on a hole.

FACE ANGLE: the position of the clubface relative to the intended line of ball flight. A square face aligns directly with the target. An open face is aligned to the right, while a closed face is aligned to the left.

FADE: a controlled shot that curves gently from left to right.

FAIRWAY: the grass surface running from tee to green.

FAT SHOT: shot in which the club strikes the ground before hitting the ball. Fat shots tend to create divots.

FLAT LIE: when your ball rests on a level spot in the fairway or around the green.

FLAT SWING: a swing plane that's too horizontal.

FLEX: see shaft flex.

FOOTPRINT: a buried lie in a sand bunker, where the ball has landed in someone's footprint.

FRIED EGG: a buried lie in a sand bunker, where most of the ball is below the surface of the sand. Visually, the ball looks like a "fried egg," hence the term.

FULL SWING: the longest swing you can make.

GREEN: the short-cut area around the hole, where you do your putting.

GREENS IN REGULATION: the number of times in a round in which you reach the green. (On a par-3 hole in one shot, a par-4 in two shots, and a par-5 in three or fewer shots.)

GRIP: the position of the hands on the handle of the club. Also the term for the handle of the club.

HANDICAP: the number assigned to a player's ability level, measured as a number of strokes over or under par the player is expected to play. The lower the handicap, the better the player. The handicap system allows players of differing abilities to compete on a level playing field.

HANDS ACTION: a phrase to describe a swing that relies too much upon wrist action to generate power. Also called handsy.

HOOK: a shot that starts right of the target and curves uncontrollably to the left.

HOSEL: where the shaft meets the head on a golf club.

INSIDE-OUT: swing path in which the club approaches the ball from inside the ball line moving outside the ball line after impact. An inside path usually produces pushes, hooks, or draws.

LAUNCH ANGLE: the angle of a ball's flight immediately after it leaves the clubface.

LIE: the position of the ball on the ground. Also, in clubfitting terms, the lie is the angle formed between the shaft and clubhead.

LOFT: the angle of the clubface. Also refers to the amount of height a shot achieves.

LPGA: Ladies Professional Golf Association.

OPEN FACE: the clubface turns right at address or strikes the ball to the right at impact, usually producing a shot that lands to the right of the target.

OUTSIDE-IN: swing path in which the club approaches the ball from outside the ball line moving inside the ball line after impact. An outside path produces pulls, fades or slices, depending on the position of the clubface at impact.

OVER THE TOP: a swing motion where a player brings the club down on a too-vertical plane. Typically caused by too-upright posture. See upright swing.

PAR: the expected score on any given hole, based on its length and difficulty.

PGA: Professional Golfers' Association.

PIVOT: the rotation of the body during the swing.

PLAYING ZONE: my term for the angle created by imaginary lines drawn from the ball at address, up through the shaft through the right hip and from the ball up through the right shoulder. The area between these two lines is the Playing Zone, and keeping your swing plane within this area produces playable ball flight.

PRACTICE GREEN: an area set aside for working on your putting.

PULL: a shot that follows a straight path to the left of the target.

PUSH: a shot that follows a straight path to the right of the target.

PUTTER: the straight-faced club used on the putting greens.

READ THE GREEN: to determine the path a putt must travel to reach the hole.

ROUGH: the grass bordering the fairways that is taller and generally more unforgiving than the fairway. The rough may also be present near greens, tees, and bunkers.

SAND SAVE: when you get up and down from a greenside bunker and the final score on that hole is par.

SAND TRAP: a bunker filled with sand.

SHAFT: the part of the club that joins the grip to the clubhead.

SHAFT FLEX: term used to express the relative bending properties of a golf club shaft. A flexible shaft, obviously, bends more than a super-stiff shaft (also called a Tour-stiff shaft).

SHANK: a shot struck in the hosel area of the golf club, resulting in a flight path far right of the target.

SIDEHILL LIE: where the ball's lie is either above or below your feet.

SLICE: a shot that starts left of the target and curves uncontrollably to the right.

STANCE: the position of the feet before a shot.

SWING PLANE: the path the club follows during the swing.

SWING THOUGHT: a simple phrase encompassing the many lessons you've learned about swing mechanics. Meant to free your mind of clutter and enable you to swing in a cohesive sequence of motion.

TAKEAWAY: see backswing.

TEMPO: the relative speed of your swing. Also called timing.

TOE LINE: see bodyline.

TOE OF THE CLUB: the end of the clubhead, farthest from the shaft.

TOE SHOT: term used when a player hits the ball on the toe of the club, usually resulting in a shorter-than-desired shot as well as one going to the right of the intended target.

UP AND DOWN: the situation in which a player misses the green and then makes one chip and one putt to achieve his score. Also called up and in.

UPRIGHT SWING: to swing with a steep vertical plane, often caused by a too-upright posture.

WAGGLE: pre-shot movement in which a golfer draws the club away from the ball a time or two, usually to relieve tension.

WRIST SET: the slight angle created by the hands and forearms at the top of the backswing. Also called wrist cock.

INDEX

alignment 34-36

backswing 45-50

   see also takeaway

Ball Flight Laws 10

ball position 17-19, 33-34

Bell, Peggy Kirk xvii

Bent Tree Golf & Country
Club xvi

Cheves, Joe 2, 140, 151

chipping 72-76

   drills:

      eyes-closed drill 75

      handkerchief
drill 75

club fitting. see equipment

Cole, Julie xii, 64, 80, 160-161

disabilities/injuries/special
considerations:

   feet problems 30

   hip problems 30

   knee problems 30

   those with eye glasses 32

downswing 51-53

drills:

   to develop "touch" 110

   see also chipping, pitching,
putting, sand shots, and swing

Duval, David 12, 114

equipment 143-150

   getting fitted 148-149

   where to get fitted 146-147

Faldo, Nick 155

Five Lessons: The Modern
Fundamentals of Golf (book) 41

"flying elbow" 12-14, 48

fundamentals 23-38

Golf My Way (book) 18

grip 25-30

   errors 28-30

   for sand shots 65

   interlocking 28

   overlap 27-28

   pressure 29-30

Harmon, Butch 3, 155

Hogan, Ben 40-41

hooking 15-17, 57-58

instruction 133-142

   assessing your first lesson
138-139

   assessing your progress
140-141

   criteria for a good instructor
136

   finding instruction 137

   how to be a good student
139-140

interlocking grip 28

lesson progression 154-155

Lopez, Nancy xii, 21

misconceptions: 7-22

   Keep your head down. 9-12

   Keep the right elbow tucked.
12-14, 45

   Keep the left arm straight or stiff.
14-15

Don't sway; Keep your head still. 15-17
Play the ball off the forward foot. 17-19, 33
Cock the wrists. 20
Take the club straight back. 20
Keep the toe up. 20
Take the club back low and slow. 20-21
Keep the head down. 32
Myers Park Country Club *xvi*
Nicklaus, Jack 18
O'Meara, Mark 155
overlap grip 27-28
Patton, Billy Joe 21
physical fitness 115-132
  cardiovascular conditioning 127-129
  Dana's personal routine 126
  nutrition & diet 129-130
  rest & renewal 130-131
  strength training 121-127
  stretching & the warm up 117-121
pitching 76-78
  drills:
    eyes-closed drill 75
    garbage can drill 79
    handkerchief drill 75
    one-handed drill 71
posture 30-32

practice 103-114
  program for weekend player 105-107
  program for aspiring amateur 107-109
  program for aspiring Tour player 110-114
pre-shot routine 95-102
  data collection 96-97
  the setup 98-99
  shot shaping 99-100
  post-shot routine 100-101
putting 80-92
  reading greens 86-88
  drills:
    blade behind the ball drill 89
    circle drill 90
    club behind the hole drill 89
    ladder drill 90
    one-hand putting drill 89
    short putt drill 89
Q-School experience *xv-xvi*, 1-2
reverse pivot 16, 59
sand shots 65-71
  ball position 68
  buried lie 69
  downhill lie 70-71
  uphill lie 70
  drills:
    one-handed drill 71
    Styrofoam cup drill 71

short game 63-94
    chipping 72-76
    pitching 76-78
    practice routine 107, 109,
        111-113
    putting 80-92
    sand shots 65-71
    the clock 66
slicing 12-14, 58
Sorenstam, Annika 12, 114
stance 30-31
    for sand shots 65
swing 39-62
    common errors:
        flat swing 57-58
        reverse pivot 59
        upright swing 58
    downswing 51-53
    follow through 54-55
    impact 53-54
    middle of the backswing
        48
    Playing Zone 41, 42, 43,
        44
    practice routine 106, 109,
        111-113

    swing plane 40-41
    takeaway 45-47
    top of the backswing 49-
        50, 51
    drills:
        belt-buckle drill 47
        broom drill 61
        feet-together drill 61
        proper width drill 51
        right-forearm
           drill 60
swing thought 11, 56-57
takeaway, the 19-21, 45-47
teachers. *see* instruction
tendonitis 14, 15
*The Golf Magazine Golf Fitness
    Handbook* (book) 127
topping 9-12
Toski, Bob 26, 139
Total Conditioning for Golfers
    (book) 127
Webb, Karrie 114
Wiren, Dr. Gary 10, 127, 153, 162
Woods, Tiger 49, 64, 155

ABOUT THE AUTHOR

Dana Rader is Director of Golf at Ballantyne Resort in Charlotte, North Carolina and President of the Dana Rader Golf School, which instructs more than 7,000 students a year. She is a GOLF *Magazine* Top 100 Instructor and was named one of America's Top 50 Teachers by *Golf Digest* in 2000. She frequently appears on The Golf Channel and Golf Academy Live and routinely contributes to national sports magazines, including GOLF *Magazine, Golf for Women* and *Sports Illustrated.* A recipient of numerous awards from golf and business organizations, Rader was the 1990 LPGA Teacher of the Year.

Scott Martin, who assisted with the manuscript, lived in Canada and England before attending the University of North Carolina as a Morehead Scholar. He is the author of *The Insiders' Guide to Golf in the Carolinas* and contributes regularly to national and regional publications. In 2002, he won the Carolinas Golf Reporters Association championship.

THE DANA RADER GOLF SCHOOL

Established to incorporate the best traits of the finest instructional facilities in the nation, the Dana Rader Golf School offers a variety of programs to help both new and experienced players better their games. Featuring programs on everything from the short game to the full swing, the Dana Rader Golf School employs a staff of accredited and dedicated teaching professionals.

The heart of the school is a 2,000-square-foot building, equipped with all-weather hitting bays, an indoor video/hitting room, a video library, a refreshment center, and office space. The 27-foot by 34-foot hitting room and classroom combination provides meeting space and is equipped with video equipment for student/instructor analysis. Surrounding the building is a natural outdoor hitting area and three deluxe putting and chipping greens with a practice bunker.

The school operates on the grounds of the **Ballantyne Resort Hotel**, and many golfers visiting the school choose to stay here. With European antiques, original artwork, and grand chandeliers, the resort combines old-world elegance with world-class services and amenities, including deluxe meeting facilities, exquisite dining, and one of the nation's finest spas. An extensive array of body, beauty, and therapeutic spa services complement the resort's health facilities, which include a complete fitness complex with an indoor grotto pool, two resistance pools, steam sauna, and a whirlpool.

The resort features an award-wining 18-hole, par-71 golf course with a full-service clubhouse. The Ballantyne Resort Hotel is one of a very select few destinations in the nation equipped to host corporate and vacationing guests in such splendor.

Contact Information:

The Dana Rader Golf School
10000 Ballantyne Commons Parkway
Charlotte, NC 28277
(704) 542-7635 or toll-free,
1-877-997-2337 (1-877-99-RADER)
www.danarader.com

The Ballantyne Resort Hotel
10000 Ballantyne Commons Parkway
Charlotte, NC 28277
(704) 248-4000 or toll-free, 1-866-248-4824
www.ballantyneresort.com